A JUMP START COURSE
IN C++ PROGRAMMING

D1301351

A JUMP START COURSE IN C++ PROGRAMMING

JAMES W. COOPER
RICHARD B. LAM
IBM T. J. Watson Research Center
Yorktown Heights, New York

A Wiley-Interscience Publication
JOHN WILEY & SONS, INC.
New York / Chichester / Brisbane / Toronto / Singapore

Copyright © 1994 by John Wiley & Sons, Inc.

Library of Congress Cataloging in Publication Data:

Cooper, James William, 1943–
    A jump start course in C++ programming / James W. Cooper and
Richard B. Lam.
        p.   cm.
    "A Wiley-Interscience publication."
    Includes bibliographical references.
    ISBN 0-471-03171-2 (alk. paper)
    1. C++ (Computer program language)   I. Lam, Richard B.
II. Title.
QA76.73.C153C665   1994
005.13′3—dc20   94-16755

Printed in the United States of America

10 9 8 7 6 5 4 3 2 1

CONTENTS

3 DAYS TO LEARNING C++

"Do you think that you are old enough to wed?
Will you wait until you're eighty in the shade?
The Mikado

The C++ language is fast becoming the standard for programming development, and many experienced C programmers need a way to upgrade their knowledge in this area quickly. We developed this book out of a series of three 2-hour lectures we gave a number of times for programmers and scientists who were familiar with C but had not yet learned the ins and outs of C++.

While C++ is more complex than C and is in fact a higher level language, it has much in common with C. We felt that if we could infect or "jump start" people familiar with C, they could quickly take off on their own and begin writing effective C++ programs.

This text is divided into two major parts: the jump start section and a section of advanced examples. To be successful in learning C++, we recommend that you have some reasonable familiarity with the C language. Then, we suggest that you read each section on a different day and spend some time the rest of that day doing several of the exercises in that section. You will NOT become proficient in C++ just by reading: writing some actual programs is critical to your success.

Once you have completed this jump start course, you should be ready for nontrivial programming in C++. Then, take a look at some of the advanced examples in the second part of the book. Good luck and happy learning.

ACKNOWLEDGMENTS

We'd particularly like to thank Wolfgang Segmuller and David Jameson here at the Watson Research Center for first infecting us with C++ and would especially like to acknowledge helpful comments from Dave Mainey, Jean-Christophe Simon, Ed Clarke, and Ed So from IBM Research, and Dr. Charles Jonah from the Argonne National Laboratory.

We'd also like to thank our wives Vicki and Kathy for their patience during our evening and weekend determination to finish.

The brief quotes at the beginning of each chapter are all by W. S. Gilbert, from the Gilbert and Sullivan operettas. The byzantine complexity of the C language (before C++, of course) seemed to us to map rather well onto the topsy-turvy world created by these Victorians.

A JUMP START COURSE
IN C++ PROGRAMMING

DAY 1

CHAPTER 1

WHY LEARN C++?

"But I'd rather have half a mortal I DO love, than have a dozen I don't."
Iolanthe

How Do C and C++ Differ?

Let's start out our consideration of C++ with a homely analogy. Suppose you are a physical education teacher and want to make sure that every class member has 15 minutes of exercise at the beginning of each class. You don't have enough space or equipment for all class members to do the same sort of exercise, so you tell them to pick up a token from a bowl on the way in. Those with red tokens will do situps, those with yellow tokens will run around the track, those with blue tokens will climb ropes, and those with green tokens will do step aerobics.

Students come in and pick up tokens and immediately two problems occur: some students can't figure out which token means which exercise and some students are not sufficiently skilled or experienced for the exercise they have been assigned. So the next time, you decide to let students pick their own exercise based on what they know how to do. This works much better since students are doing something they do well and not trying to do something they will fail at.

Standard procedural languages like C are much like the first class, where each student function is given a token and told what it means and what to do with it, while object-oriented languages like C++ are much like the second case, where each student object is told to do "exercise" and expected to select the type of exercise that suits each best. We will see as we look at the improvements in the C++ approach that it is much simpler and more elegant. Finally, it is harder to make silly mistakes like thinking the blue token means situps, which could easily lead to a "software crash."

3

Why Should I Learn C++?

You might ask why you should even bother to learn C++, since thousands of complex, successful programs have been written in C. What does C++ add and is it worth the pain of learning yet another language?

First let's start by remembering the pain and difficulty of learning C itself. C is a fairly low level language with

- turgid syntax,

```
a = b ? c < d :e;
```

- confusing symbols,

```
if (c->d != e)
```

- very little error checking,

```
float x[100];
x[100] = 12.0;   /* boom! */
```

- confusing input and output,

```
printf ("%d", i);
scanf ("%d", &i);
```

and pointers, pointers, and more pointers. Pointers are, in fact, the one thing in C that most likely drives programmers to drink. They can be endlessly confusing and are continually required in creating and calling functions.

Is C++ an Improvement?

C++ is definitely easier to program in. The syntax is similar to C itself and is a superset of C. However, C++ allows you to use symbols as operators on new data types, provides more type and error checking, and has a simpler input and output system.

Most important, for many common operations, you can just about forget about pointers! Convinced yet?

If you aren't convinced, let's take you through the stages of acceptance people usually go through with C++. Some of these follow from a list given by Eckel:

1. Denial. You reject the idea of the need to learn YAL (yet another language!)

2. Grudging acceptance of improvements over C. You begin to recognize the advantages of the features in C++ that make programming easier than it was in C.

3. Vague understanding of classes as objects. You begin to see what objects might actually be used for.

4. Denial of function overloading. The idea of giving several functions the same name seems an anathema at first.

5. Appreciation of information hiding. You begin to see the advantages of hiding implementation details.

6. Appreciation of inheritance. You begin to see that classes inheriting properties from each other can simplify your job.

7. Appreciation of virtual keyword. You see how you can actually use this crucial feature.

8. Disdain of all other languages and acceptance of C++ as a minor deity. You have become a true C++ evangelist and bigot!

Congratulations on your conversion to the True Way.

Just as our physical education teacher did, you will begin to find that C++ imparts more structure to the way you write programs and prevents you from making foolish or dangerous errors. C++ is actually simpler to learn and use than C was, once you rearrange your thinking to the C++ object-oriented style. In this style each object (or class or structure) contains both data and functions or *methods* specifically designed for the requirements of that object. So, when you tell an object to perform a function such as "exercise," it will select the approach appropriate for that kind of data. This in itself is the fundamental strength of the C++ approach, as we will see in the chapters that follow.

The Example Diskette

All of the example programs in this book are provided on the accompanying diskette. A complete list of these programs and instructions for their use is given in Appendix B.

References

1. B. Stroustrup, *The C++ Programming Language,* second edition, Addison-Wesley, Murray Hill, 1991.

2. M. Ellis and B. Stroustrup, *The Annotated C++ Reference*, Addison-Wesley, Murray Hill, 1990.

3. S. B. Lippman, *C++ Primer, 2nd edition*, Addison-Wesley, Reading, MA, 1991

4. B. Eckel, *C++ Inside and Out*, Osborne-McGraw-Hill, Berkeley, 1993.

CHAPTER 2

HOW C++ IMPROVES UPON C

"I was the beau ideal of the morbid young esthetical--
To doubt my inspiration was regarded as heretical,
Until you cut me out with your placidity emetical.
Patience

In this chapter, we'll outline some of tbe main differences between C and C++.
We will see that, at the very least, C++ is a better form of the base C language.

Function Prototypes

Unlike C, C++ is a strongly typed language. Every function you write *must* have
a function prototype that describes the type and number of arguments. For
example, if you have a routine **quadcalc** that returns a float and takes three inputs
as floats, you must have the declaration

```
float quadcalc(float a, float b, float c);
```

appear ahead of the first call to the function. In small, one-module programs, you
can put this declaration at the beginning of the program code. In larger
multiple-module programs you usually put it in a separate header (.h) file. The
one exception to this rule is if the function code appears in the file before it is
called. Then the function itself becomes the prototype.

While it is true that C as defined by the American National Standards Institute
(ANSI) allows this type checking, it is optional and there is no penalty for leaving
it out.

The const Declaration

In C, the only way to provide a constant value is to use the **#define** statement:

```
#define PI 3.1416
```

7

In C++, you can now use the **const** declaration to indicate that a variable may not have its value changed:

```
const double pi = 3.1416;
```

This method creates an actual memory location containing data. It has an address and can have a pointer pointing to it. This is far more robust than simply having the C preprocessor replace all occurrences of **PI** with 3.146 and avoids the sort of errors these **#define** declarations can lead to. In a significant change from C, you can use these constants in dimensioning arrays:

```
const int dim = 100;
float x[dim];
```

While ANSI C does allow the **const** declaration, only C++ allows you to declare arrays in this way.

Comments

C++ introduces the one-line comment beginning with the double slash:

```
x = y + z;        //compute value of x
```

The standard comment surrounded by /* and */ remains as well:

```
a = b - c;        /* standard C comment */
```

The advantage of this new comment structure is that it is safer when you want to comment out a single line which itself contains a comment:

```
// a = b - c;    /* line commented out */
```

The // comment supercedes the C-style comment and removes that line from the compiled code.

Enumerated Types

C introduced the *enumerated type*, which is a way of assigning a series of constant names to a data type:

```
enum color { black, blue, green, red, yellow, white}
```

Then you can declare variables of that type:

```
enum color foregnd, backgnd;
```

The variables **foregnd** and **backgnd** can take on the values **black** through **white**, which the compiler assigns as integer values 0 through 5.

```
foregnd  = red;
backgnd = black;
```

However, the C compiler also allows you to use the integer values directly, leading to some confusion:

```
foregnd = 3;              /* red   */
backgnd = 0;              /* black */
```

By contrast, in C++, there are two differences. First, the declaration of variables of an enumerated type need not be preceded by the keyword **enum**:

```
color foregnd, backgnd;
```

Second, if you attempt to assign an integer value to an enumerated type variable, the compiler will warn you that this may be an error:

```
color = 4;        //compiler warning generated
```

Function Calls by Reference

In C, if you wanted to pass a variable to a function in such a way that the function could alter that variable, you had to pass a pointer to the variable and return the value through the pointer:

```
void quadcalc (float a, float b, float c, float *x)
   {
   *x = -b + sqrt(b*b - 4*a*c)/(2*a);
   }
```

Then, each time you called the function, you had to remember to pass in a pointer value:

```
quadcalc( a, b, c, &x);
```

C++ introduces the call by reference. This method allows you to use the ampersand to specify in the function header (and prototype) that the variable is to be passed by reference:

```
void quadcalc (float a, float c, float& x)
   {
   x = -b + sqrt(b*b - 4*a*c)/(2*a);
   }
```

You do not need to mark the return variable within the function in any special way: the compiler will take care of generating the requisite code. You can then call this function without having to remember to mark the value to be passed by reference in any special way. The compiler will generate the correct code, passing **x** by reference:

```
quadcalc(a, b, c, x);
```

This completely eliminates the need for continuous, low-level use of pointers in day-to-day programming and leaves this dirty work to the compiler. Note that such pointers may *not* be null. This method is, in fact, the *preferred* way to pass large structures and class instances to functions, since the entire structure need not be copied onto the stack each time it is used.

Inline Functions Replace Macros

In C, if you want to write a simple function to be inserted in-line in the code, you used an expanded form of the **#define** statement which generated a macro by replacement:

```
#define cube(x) x*x*x
```

Then each time you write a statement like

```
y = cube(a);
```

the preprocessor replaces it with

```
y = a*a*a;
```

However, if you write

```
y = cube(a++);
```

this expands to

```
a = 4;
y = a++ * a++ *a++;
```

which evaluates to 120 instead of 64, and **a** will return with the value 7 instead of 5. In addition, because of C's weaker type checking, there is nothing to prevent you from writing

```
char a;
a = 'q';
y = cube(a);
```

and since characters convert to integers, this too would evaluate to some unexpected result.

To prevent this nonsense from occurring, C++ introduces the **inline** function:

```
inline float cube(float x)
{
 y = x * x * x;
 return(y);
}
```

The **inline** keyword represents a request to the compiler to insert this function's code in-line as the code is generated, to prevent the overhead of a function call and return. The compiler is not required to honor these requests and generally will not for larger or more complex functions. However, type checking is retained and a statement like

```
char a;
a = 'q';
y =cube(a);
```

would generate an error message. Further,

```
y =  cube(a++);
```

will evaluate correctly.

Function Arguments

C++ allows you to specify default values for arguments passed to functions. Then if you omit these values when you call the function, the default values are used instead. For example, you could write an error message routine, and realizing that one error message is very common and will be called from many places in your code, you could write

```
void errmesg(char mesg[] = "Printer offline")
{
cout << mesg;
}
```

Then if you called the routine with

```
errmesg("Drive door open");
```

you would get the drive door message, but if you called it with

```
errmesg();
```

you would get the "printer off line" error message.

You can do the same thing with multiple-argument functions:

```
float expon(float a, int y=2);
```

You cannot intermingle passed values and default values: the default values must be the last ones in the argument list.

Memory Management

When you need to allocate memory in C, you must use the **malloc** and **free** functions. For example, if you need space for the structure

```
struct fi
   {
   int a;
   float b;
   };
```

you allocate a pointer,

```
struct fi *pfi;
```

call **malloc** to allocate memory,

```
pfi = (struct fi *) malloc(sizeof(struct fi));
```

and call **free** to release the memory,

```
free(pfi);
```

In C++, you can instead use the **new** and **delete** operators, which are much simpler and do not require the complex type casting:

```
fi *pfi = new fi;        //allocate memory
      // code goes here
delete pfi;              //release memory
```

In a similar fashion, if you want to allocate an array of data, in C you would write

```
int *p;
p = (int *) malloc(100 * sizeof(int));
```

```
        /* ... code goes here */
    free(p);
```

In C++, we use the **new** statement followed by the type and the dimensions in brackets:

```
    int p* = new int[100];

        //...code goes here...
    delete p;
```

You can also allocate memory for structures this way:

```
struct NameFloat
{
  float *f;    //floating point number
  char *name; //name of field
};

NameFloat *nf = new NameFloat[100];
```

This array can be deleted by

```
    delete [] nf;
```

Note the brackets preceding the pointer name. The statement

```
    delete nf;
```

would deallocate the memory the pointer refers to, but if the pointer points to a structure which itself contains pointers (such as **char *name**), that memory will only be released if you specify the brackets as part of the **delete** statement. We'll see how this occurs when we talk about destructors in the following chapter.

One important stylistic difference between C and C++ is that it is usual to declare and allocate variables where they are first used rather than at the top of the routine. This can be important when some logical paths through the routine will result in some memory allocation and deallocation statements being skipped: in this case the program could run faster than if the memory is always allocated.

Input and Output

In C, if you want to read in and print out values, you use the **scanf** and **printf** functions:

```
#include <stdio.h>
```

```
float x, y;
scanf("%f", &x);        /* read in x        */
y = x*x;                /* do some math     */
printf("y= %f \n", y);  /* print out result */
```

These functions suffer from confusing syntax: the format string is complex, and the need for pointers in **scanf** but not in **printf** confuses many a programmer.

In C++, there is a new class of input and output functions, called stream functions, defined in the standard C++ header file **iostream.h**. For simple programs, these functions are much easier to use:

```
#include <iostream.h>
float x,y;

cin >> x;                       //read in x
y = x* x;                       //do some math
cout << "y=" << y <<endl;       //print out result
```

The keyword **cin** refers to the input stream or "standard in." The ">>" symbol used in this context is called the *extraction operator*: it extracts characters from the input stream.

Similarly, **cout** refers to "standard out," and the "<<" symbol is called the *insertion operator*: it inserts characters into the output stream. Finally, the keyword **endl** represents the end of line character "\n" and also flushes the output buffer so that all characters currently ready for output are printed. Note that both **cin** and **cout** appear first on the line, followed by the list of data to receive or provide values.

C programmers may find these new uses of "<<" and ">>" surprising. However, they still retain their previous meanings for integers: shift left and shift right. Both are allowed in C++, where the context determines the meaning. This is called *operator overloading*.

In addition, the data types of the values operated on by **cin** and **cout** include all the standard C++ data types. Thus **cin** and **cout** are themselves overloaded, producing the correct type of data conversion for each data type: **int, float, long, double, char,** and **string**.

Exception Handling

C++ introduces built-in methods of handling exceptions such as
- division by zero
- numerical overflow
- out of memory

The occurrence of an exception is called *throwing*, and for each exception there will be a throw expression to transfer control to the exception handler. The exception handlers are said to *catch* the exceptions. As of this writing, only a few compilers have implemented this feature. We will discuss it in the advanced examples section of this book. You should be sure to look up the implementation details in your compiler's manual.

ANSI C Holdovers

The C language has developed over a period of more than 10 years and a large number of programmers still program in a C style closely related to the original specifications. The ANSI standards committee has established newer standards for C that inherit a number of the best ideas from C++.

However, since C compilers must support the original C style and features, many of these newer ideas are either seldom used or optional:

- ANSI C supports function prototypes just as C++ does.
- ANSI C supports the **const** declaration, but it is seldom used over **#define**.

In addition, ANSI C and C++ both support the function prototype for a function with a variable number of arguments. For example, the **printf** statement always has a string format argument followed by any number of individual arguments. The function prototype for **printf** indicates this with the ellipsis symbols:

```
void printf(char *,...);
```

ANSI C and C++ also support the concept of volatile data types:

```
volatile int comport;
```

The **volatile** keyword indicates the variable that follows may be changed by some function outside the current one, such as an interrupt service routine or a signal handler. Since the compiler cannot assume that a value of a volatile variable copied into a register will always remain valid, it does not optimize any references to it and thus always fetches the variable from memory.

Not all current C++ or C compilers implement **volatile** completely. You should check with your compiler reference manual.

CHAPTER 3

STRUCTURES AND CLASSES

"When next your Houses do assemble. You will tremble."
"Oh, spare us."
Iolanthe

Let's start out our investigation of object-oriented programming by considering a simple C structure representing a rectangle:

```
#include <iostream.h>
struct rectangle
  {
  float height;        //height of the rectangle
  float width;         //width of the rectangle
  int xpos;            //x position on the screen
  int ypos;            //y position on the screen
} ;
```

Note that this structure definition includes a height and width and values for the x and y position on the screen. Note also that the structure definition always terminates with a semicolon. Now, if we would like to draw this rectangle on the screen, we would write a simple routine called **drawrect**. In this case, to keep our examples simple, we will just print out the values of the x and y position and call this "drawing." We have included the header file **iostream.h** so we can use the convenient C++ **cout** object. We also will make immediate use of the convenient new & symbol to indicate that the **rc** structure is passed by reference rather than by value:

```
void drawrect(rectangle&  rc)
{
 cout << "position is " << rc.ypos << rc.xpos;
}
```

In addition to the **drawrect** function, we will also need functions to initialize the rectangle structure, position it, and move it. These are shown below:

```
void initrect(rectangle& rc, float h, float w)
```

```
{
      rc.height= h;         //set height
      rc.width = w;         //and width
      rc.xpos = 0;          //and initialize position
      rc.ypos = 0;          //to 0,0
}
 // --------------------------------------------------
void posnrect(rectangle& rc, int x, int y)
  {
  rc.xpos = x              //posiiton rectangle to x,y
  rc.ypos = y;
  }
 // --------------------------------------------------
void moverect(rectangle& rc, int dx, int dy)
  {
   rc.xpos += dx;          //move rectangle by dx,dy
   rc.ypos += dy;
  }
```

With these functions, we can then write a simple program to initialize a rectangle, position it, draw it, and then move it and redraw it. This program might look like

```
void main ()
  {
  rectangle rc;                //declare rectangle structure
  initrect(rc, 3.0,2.0);       //create a 2 x 3 rectangle
  posnrect(rc, 100,10);        //set corner at 100,100
  drawrect(rc);                //draw the rectangle
  moverect(rc, 50,50)          //move it by 50 pixels
  drawrect(rc);                //draw the rectangle again
  }
```

Changing the Drawing Function

Now, in general, we do not know how to actually draw a rectangle for any type of operating system and display. We don't know what other drawing parameters might be needed, such as pointers to presentation spaces, line types, and widths.

So, if we can make the drawing routine part of the structure describing the rectangle, we can change or add parameters as needed without changing the actual calling program. So, as our first step towards object-oriented programming, we will rewrite out drawing routine as a *member function* of the rectangle structure:

```
struct rectangle    //rectangle and drawing routine
  {
  float height;                //height and width
  float width;
  int xpos;                    //x and y position
  int ypos;
  void draw();                 //drawing function
```

```
};
```

We have shown the drawing function within the structure as a function prototype. The actual drawing routine is shown below:

```
void rectangle::draw()
{
  cout << "position is " << ypos <<" "<< xpos << "\n";
}
```

Now we see that the prototype of a *member function* generally appears within the structure definition and that the actual function usually appears later, below. As this is a member function, it is written out with the structure name preceding it:

```
void rectangle::draw()
```

The double colon between the structure name and the member function name is called the *scoping operator*. Since we can only call this member function as part of the rectangle structure, we don't need to include the **rect** structure name as part of the member function and can call the function **draw** instead of **drawrect**.

To call a member function, we refer to it just as if it were a variable inside the structure:

```
      rc.draw();
```

The data it uses are part of the rectangle structure **rc** and do not need to be passed to the function specifically. Further, if we change or add parameters to the rectangle structure, we don't have to change any of the calls to the member functions, since they can refer to the structure variables directly. Our complete main program now becomes

```
void main ()
{
rectangle rc;           //declare rectangle structure
initrect(rc, 3.0,2.0);  //create a 2 x 3 rectangle
posnrect(rc, 100,100);  //set corner at 100,100
rc.draw();              //draw the rectangle
moverect(rc, 50,50);    //move it by 50 pixels
rc.draw();              //draw the rectangle
}
```

Adding Other Member Functions

Not surprisingly, you can rewrite the position and move functions to become member functions in the same way:

```
struct rectangle
{
float height;
float width;
int xpos;
int ypos;
void draw();                 //draw member function
void posn(int x, int y);     //position member function
void move( int x, int y);    //move member function
};
```

These two new functions are written as

```
void rectangle::posn(int x, int y)
{
 xpos = x;
 ypos = y;
}
/*-------------------------------------------------------*/
void rectangle::move(int dx, int dy)
{
 xpos += dx;
 ypos += dy;
}
```

with the rectangle structure name preceding them and the :: scoping operator defining the structure of which they are a member. Our new main calling program then becomes

```
void main ()
{
 rectangle rc;
 initrect(rc, 3.0,2.0); //create a 2 x 3 rectangle
 rc.posn( 100,100);     //set corner at 100,10
 rc.draw();             //draw it
 rc.move( 50,50);       //move it by 50 pixels
 rc.draw();             //draw it again
}
```

Note that our program has been simplified significantly: none of the member functions require any rectangle arguments and the program actually has become more readable with the simpler function names.

The Rectangle Constructor

Now, obviously, we should not have to write a rectangle initialization function like **initrect**, either. We should be able to make this a member function as well. However in C++, this member function which initializes the structure is called a **constructor,** and it is called automatically whenever a new instance of that structure is created. The constructor is a function with the same name as the structure itself and it has no return type (such as **void** or **int**). Our structure with the constructor prototype is

```
struct rectangle
{
 float height;
 float width;
 int xpos;
 int ypos;
 rectangle(float h, float w);
 void draw();
 void posn(int x, int y);
 void move( int x, int y);
};
```

and the actual code for the constructor is

```
rectangle::rectangle( float h, float w)
{                         //rectangle constructor
 height= h;               //initialize height
 width = w;               //and width
 xpos = 0;                //and set the position to 0,0
 ypos = 0;
}
```

Note that the constructor takes initialization arguments and can set additional internal variables to default values as well. The constructor is called when the structure instance is declared, so you must supply these arguments as you create the structure:

```
        rectangle rc(3.0, 2.0);
```

The complete object-oriented version of our simple program is

```
void main ()
{
rectangle rc(3.0, 2.0);      //declare a 3 x 2 rectangle
rc.posn( 100,100);           //set corner at 100,100
rc.draw();
rc.move( 50,50);             //move it by 50 pixels
rc.draw();
}
```

While it is conventional in C++ to provide a constructor, if you do not, the compiler generates a default constructor for you. A default constructor does not, of course, initialize any instance's internal variables or allocate any memory for arrays.

Information Hiding

So far, we have simply created a somewhat more advanced form of a **struct** with functions embedded in it. All of the members of this structure are still accessible to any part of the program and to any function the program or subsequent users write. We would prefer that the program not be able to access any of these internal variables. C++ introduces the **public** and **private** keywords to make this information hiding possible:

```
struct rectangle {
private:
   float height;            //private internal variables
float width;
   int xpos;
   int ypos;
public:
   rectangle(float h, float w); //constructor
   void draw();                 //draw functions
   void posn(int x, int y);     //position function
   void move( int x, int y);    //move function
};
```

   In this version of the structure, the internal variables *height*, *width*, *xpos*, and *ypos* are hidden from the rest of the program and are only accessible to the member functions. Only the functions themselves are accessible to code in the remainder of the program. As we have shown in this simple case, all of the member functions are public and all of the variables are private. You can also write programs in which some of the member functions are themselves private. This means that such functions are accessible only *to other member functions in that structure*, and not to the rest of the program. Usually, you make all the variables private in any case.

The C++ Class

In C++, as you may already realize, we don't really make much use of *structures*, but we make a lot of use of *classes*. And what, you might ask, is the difference between a **struct** and a **class**? There is practically no difference. The **struct** has all of its members public by default, and the class has all of its members private by default. If we had created a rectangle **class** instead of a **struct**, we would have written

```
class rectangle
{
  float height;               //internal variables
  float width;                //default to private
  int xpos;
  int ypos;
```

```
public:
  rectangle(float h, float w); //constructor
  void draw();                 //public member functions
  void posn(int x, int y);
  void move( int x, int y);
```

It is conventional, however, to include the **private** keyword in classes, since larger classes may have several private and public sections. Further, many programmers list the public sections of a class first since those are the ones which someone reading the code would need to understand:

```
class rectangle
{
 public:
  rectangle(float h, float w); //constructor
  void draw();                 //public member functions
  void posn(int x, int y);
  void move( int x, int y);
 private:
  float height;                //internal variables
  float width;                 //default to private
  int xpos;
  int ypos;
};
```

Needless to say, we will use **class**es henceforth instead of **struct**s. We refer to variables of type **class** as *instances* of a class or as *objects*. The functions inside the class are referred to as *member functions*.

Class-based Programming

Now let's look at what we have described here. We've created an entirely new programming style where data and functions co-exist inside a class and where functions are called *without passing any data to them*. This stylistic change is a very significant part of programming in C++: the parameters that you would normally pass into C functions are already inside the class with the functions. Thus, there is far less chance of misusing functions by passing them the wrong data or confusing pointers to one data set with pointers to another similar data set. The net result is that C++ programs are simpler to write and simpler to read. We'll be expanding on how this programming style can be used to write more error-free programs in the chapters that follow.

CHAPTER 4

CONSTRUCTORS AND DESTRUCTORS

"Peers will teem in Christendom, and a Duke's exalted station... Be attainable by competitive examination."
Iolanthe

Constructors

As we have seen, every class has a constructor associated with it. If you do not write a specific constructor to initialize the private variables, the compiler generates a default constructor for you.

You can also have more than one constructor in a class, as long as each has a different list of arguments or function "signature." For example, you could have two rectangle constructors, one with height and width arguments and one with no arguments:

```
rectangle(float h, float w); //with arguments
rectangle();                 //without arguments
```

Then, our first constructor is implemented as before:

```
rectangle::rectangle( float h, float w)
{
 height= h;
 width = w;
 xpos = 0;
 ypos = 0;
}
```

and our new constructor assigns a default height and width:

```
rectangle::rectangle()
{
 height= 10;
 width = 10;
 xpos = 0;
 ypos = 0;
```

```
}
```
Then you can call either of them, depending on how you declare each class instance:

```
rectangle r1(120, 130); //uses first constructor
rectangle r2;            //uses default constructor
```

Note that in this second case, parentheses are not used.

Destructors

Just as you may need to initialize variables with a constructor, you may need to "clean up" when a particular class instance is no longer needed. A destructor function is called automatically when an object goes "out of scope." This happens when

- the function ends
- the program ends
- a block containing temporary variables ends
- a **delete** operator is called

However, whenever a class contains a pointer to memory you allocate, it is your responsibility to release the memory before the class instance is destroyed. Otherwise the memory *containing* the pointer will be released but the memory the pointer points to will remain allocated but inaccessible. A destructor function has the same name as the class but is preceded by a tilde (~):

```
~rectangle();
```

Destructors have no arguments, return no values, and are never called directly. They are called automatically when a class instance goes out of scope.

Let's consider a simple string class:

```
class string
{
private:
   char *s;                 //string pointer
   int size;                //and length are private
public:
   string(char *);          //constructor
   ~string();               //destructor
   void print();
};
```

This class contains a pointer to an array of **char** and a variable containing the actual string length, so we needn't recalculate it each time we need it. Since we need to allocate memory for the array for each instance, the constructor for this string class would probably be something like

```
string::string(char *c)          //constructor
{
  s = new char[strlen(c)+1];     //allocate string
  strcpy(s, c);                  //copy string
  size = strlen(s);              //store size
}
```

We must allocate **strlen(c) + 1** bytes since the **strlen** function returns the length of the null-terminated string *minus* the null byte. Since we need that null byte in order to manipulate this internally as a string, we need to allocate space for it.

Since this class contains a pointer which points to memory which we allocate during the constructor, we must have a destructor as well:

```
string::~string()               //destructor
{
delete s;                       //de-allocate memory
}
```

Note that brackets preceding the array name in the delete statement

```
delete [] s;
```

are not necessary here. Brackets indicate that destructors must be called for each member of the array. These are needed only when **s** is an array of classes, each of which contains pointers which must be deallocated. A complete version of this simple program is shown below:

```
#include <iostream.h>
#include <string.h>
//----------string class definition----------------
class string
{
 private:
   char *s;                 //string pointer
   int size;                //and length are private
 public:
   string(char *);          //constructor
   ~string();               //destructor
   void print();
};

string::string(char *c)   //constructor

{
  s = new char[strlen(c)+1];    //allocate memory
```

```
  strcpy(s, c);                    //copy string
  size = strlen(s);                //store size
}

string::~string()          //destructor
{
  delete s;                //de-allocate memory
}

void string::print()
{
  cout << s <<endl;
}


//---main program for illustrating string class---
void main()
{
  string a("abcd");               //call constructor
  a.print();                      //print
}                                 //call destructor
```

CHAPTER 5

A SIMPLE EXAMPLE OF INHERITANCE

"Your honor had an elder brother?
It had.
Who should have inherited your title and, with it, its curse?
Aye. "
Ruddigore

When we wrote the rectangle class, we created member functions to operate on the rectangle named **draw**, **move**, and **posn**. We can create similar functions for any other class, since these functions are really tied to the class definition. Thus, we could write a new class having these same member functions without any conflict.

Let's create a new class called **square** containing these same functions. After we have written it, we'll see how we could derive the **square** class from the **rectangle** class. As before, the square class needs a constructor and **move**, **posn**, and **draw** functions:

```
class square
{
  float side;
  int xpos, ypos;
  public:
    square(float s);          //constructor
    void move(int x, int y);       //move square
    void posn(int x, int y);       //position square
    void draw();              //draw square
};
// ----------------------------
square::square(float s)          //constructor
{
  side =s;                  //set side length
}

void square::move(int x, int y) //move square
{
  xpos+=x;
  ypos+=y;
```

```
}

void square::posn(int x, int y) //position on page
{
 xpos=x;
 ypos=y;
}

void square::draw()                    //simple drawing function
{
 cout << "x ="<<xpos<<" y = "<< ypos << endl;
}

// ----------------------------
void main ()
{
   square sq(5);            //declare square size
   sq.posn(40,60);          //position it
   sq.draw();               //draw it
   sq.move(10,10);          //move it
   sq.draw();          //draw it again
}
```

In addition, just as we created multiple constructors for a single class, we can create several member functions having the same name as long as they have a different argument signature. Here we show a second version having only one argument:

```
void square::move(int dxy)
{
 xpos += dxy;             //move same amount in both x and y
 ypos += dxy;
}
```

Then, if you called **move** with two arguments, the first one would be invoked, but if you called

```
        sq.move(5);
```

the single argument version of **move** would be called, moving the square the same amount in both directions. Again, these multiple constructors can be used primarily to improve program legibility and clarity. As with any other language, you could use features like this to completely obfuscate your program, but we strongly recommend you avoid "cute programming arabesques" that might lead to such confusion.

Specifying Member Functions in the Class Definition

Thus far, we have shown a function prototype inside the class and the actual function implementation after the class definition. It is also perfectly legal to simply write the function code right inside the class definition:

```
struct rectangle {
  private:
    float height;
    float width;
    int xpos;
    int ypos;
  public:
    rectangle(float h, float w)
            {height=h; width=w; xpos=ypos=0;}
    void draw(){cout << xpos<<" "<<ypos<<endl;}
    inline void posn(int x, int y){xpos=x; ypos=y;}
    void move( int x, int y){xpos +=x; ypos += y;}
};
```

This method is, of course, somewhat more turgid and less readable, but it is common for very small functions and required for those which are to be **inline** like the **posn** function above. The disadvantage is that many programmers prefer to place the class definition in a header file which is accessible to all users, while hiding the implementation elsewhere and not made publicly readable. Using this **inline** method, the entire class is exposed to the reader and to change by the programmer. Finally, not all debuggers handle this style of function syntax very well.

Inheritance

One of the great strengths of C++ is its ability to facilitate code reuse. When you create a new class that is similar but not identical to a previous one, it is common to have the new class inherit properties and member functions from the initial class. Since a square is just a special class of rectangle, let's reconsider our **square** class in this light and see how much code we might be able to reuse from the **rectangle** class. On inspection, we see that all of the member functions are actually the same except for the **square** constructor, which has one argument instead of two.

To create a class **square** based on our **rectangle** class, we write

```
class square : public rectangle
{
 public:
  square(float s);
};
```

Here, we are saying that the **square** class *inherits* variables and functions from the **rectangle** class. Thus, the **square** class utilizes the same member functions and variables as **rectangle** does.

Now, the nice thing is that the above definition of the **square** class is that it is *complete*. The **square** class does not need to have any private variables or member functions: it only needs the one constructor function. Further, the **square** constructor really does nothing but call the constructor for the **rectangle** class as follows:

```
square::square(float s):rectangle(s,s) //square constructor
   {
   }
```

This syntax says to take the argument **s** from the **square** constructor and pass it to the **rectangle** constructor as both the width and height values. Thus, even the constructor itself contains no new code: it just calls the **rectangle** constructor.

So even in our derived class program, the calls remain the same:

```
void main ()
{
   square sq(5);        //create an instance of square
   sq.posn(40,60);      //position it
   sq.draw();           //draw it
   sq.move(10,10);      //move it
   sq.draw();           //and draw it again
}
```

As you can see, a derived class can use all the public members of its base or parent class. Here we see the **square** class calling the **posn**, **draw**, and **move** member functions of the base **rectangle** class.

Public and Private Inheritance

In our example of **square** inheriting from **rectangle** above, we introduced the keyword **public** without comment. You will nearly always want to include this keyword when you derive one class from another: it indicates that the member functions of the derived class have access to the private members of the base class. There are two other types of inheritance: **private** and **protected**, which we will expand on later.

The Vocabulary of Inheritance

One of the more confusing parts of object-oriented nomenclature is the plethora of terms used when one object (class) inherits from another. We see terms such as

- derived and base
- parent and child
- subclass and superclass

Questions often arise: Is the the parent the precursor or the superior class? Is the subclass the original or the new class? We feel that the least ambiguity lies in using the first set of terms: *base* for the original class and *derived* for classes which inherit from it.

CHAPTER 6

A COMPLEX NUMBER CLASS

*"Two husbands have managed to acquire three wives. That's two thirds
of a husband to each wife.*
Oh, Mt. Vesuvius! Here we are in arithmetic!"
The Gondoliers

Now that we have gone over the fundamentals of class construction, let's
construct a class for complex number handling from scratch. We could start by
assuming that the internal parts of the class will be

```
class complex
{
 private:
  float real, imag;
};
```

However, this is not really the best place to start. Instead, we really should
start by deciding what operations we would like to carry out within the class. In
this simple example, we might decide that the operations will be

* assignment,
```
      complex a, b;
      b = a;
```

* taking the complex conjugate, and

```
      a.conjugate();
```

* complex addition,

```
      a.sum(b);
```

We will make the **sum** operation a member function, so that we can delay
explaining how to reuse the "+" symbol for this purpose.

Thus, **sum** and **conjugate** are our member functions and should be defined to return no values. So we write

```
class complex
{
private:
//...
public:
  void conjugate();   //operates on current class values
  void sum(complex& ); //requires two class instances
};
```

Now we write the constructors, We need to be able to initialize the values of the real and imaginary parts:

```
complex(float r, float i);
complex();                        //set default values
```

This is another example of *overloading*, where we are providing two different constructors with the same name but different arguments.

And finally, we want to be able to print out the values:

```
void print();
```

Our complete complex class declaration might look like this:

```
class complex
{
 private:
   float real, imag;           //values are private
 public:
   complex(float r, float i);   //constructor
   complex();                    //alternate constructor
   void print();                 //print values
   void conjugate();             //compute conjugate
   complex sum(complex& );       //addition
};
```

As you look at the class definition, we again remind you that constructors do not return values and they do not use the **void** keyword. Member functions, on the other hand, must return values and these must be preceded either by a type keyword or **void**. Most important, the class definition must end with a semicolon.

The Main Program

Now, without worrying about those member functions' implementation, let's write out the main program and see that we have defined the functions we actually need. In this program we will create a couple of complex numbers, take a conjugate, add the two together, and print out the result.

This program has the form

```
void main()
{
  complex a(1,2);                  //declare a
  a.print();                       //print it
  complex b(3,2);                  //declare b
  b.conjugate();                   //take complex conjugate
  b.print();
  complex c = a.sum(b);            //add them
  c.print();                       //print result
}
```

Note that we declare the complex objects *a* and *b* where we use them rather than at the top of the program. You can, of course, do this in C style as well:

```
        complex c;
        c = a.sum(b);
```

but it is usual in C++ to declare variables where we need them.

Now, we will write the member functions. We need to write the two constructors, the complex conjugate, the sum function, and the print function. The constructors are

```
complex::complex(float r, float i)      //constructor
{
  real = r;
  imag = i;
}

complex::complex()                       //default constructor
{
  real = imag = 0.0;
}
```

Remember, a constructor has the same name as the class. It is also a member function, so we precede the name with the class name resulting in the doubling of **complex::complex**. Then, if we want to create a new complex number, we simply say

```
        complex a(12.0, -4); //12 - 4i
```

If you want to create a variable which might be assigned values later, you write

```
        complex b;            //0 + 0i
```

and the default constructor will be called, assigning the real and imaginary parts to the default values of (0,0).

The complex conjugate function simply takes the negative of the imaginary part of the complex number:

```
void complex::conjugate()
{
    imag = -imag;
}
```

Since we are the "experts" here, we know how a conjugate is computed, but we have actually hidden the details of the computation from the casual user, so if we have it wrong or find a better algorithm, we could later change the conjugate functions without in any way altering the program.

The Sum Function

In our first implementation of complex addition, we will create a **sum** function, to avoid worrying about how to reuse the plus sign in this context. Our sum function just adds the real and imaginary parts and returns that complex value on the stack:

```
complex complex::sum(complex& x)
{
   return complex(real+x.real, imag+x.imag);
}
```

Here, the addition is done as part of the **return** statement. By creating a temporary complex variable as part of the return statement, we avoid using extra internal variables and worrying about whether they persist when the function terminates. We could also write this function as

```
complex complex::sum(complex x)
{
 complex y;
 y.real = real+ x.real;
 y.imag = imag+ x.imag;
 return y;
}
```

where we use an internal variable **y** and return it on the stack.

However, we must be careful in using internal variables in return statements. The following method will fail:

```
complex& complex::sum(complex x)
{
 complex y;
 y.real = real+ x.real;
 y.imag = imag+ x.imag;
```

```
  return y;
}
```

Can you see why? This version of the function returns a *pointer* to a complex number rather than a copy of the number. However, once the routine exits, the location containing *y* is no longer valid, since the memory has been dismissed, and the compiler will flag this as a warning or error.

The Print Function

The **print** function simply prints out the real and imaginary parts:

```
void complex::print()
{
cout << real << " " << imag << endl;
}
```

We are really using the **print** function as a way to inspect the contents of a class. In more elaborate classes, it is more likely that you will write **get** and **set** functions to obtain and store the contents of class instances. Remember, you never want to allow the user direct access to the internal private variables of a class.

The Complete Complex Program

```
//--------------Complex Class illustration------------
#include <iostream.h>
class complex
{
   private:
     float real, imag;          //values are private
public:
     complex(float r,float i);  //constructor
     complex();                 //alternate constructor

     complex sum(complex& );
     void print();              //print values
     void conjugate();          //compute conjugate
     };

complex::complex(float r, float i)  //constructor
{
 real= r;
 imag = i;
}

complex::complex()                       //default constructor
{
 real = imag = 0.0;
}
```

```
void complex::conjugate()          //conjugate
{
  imag = -imag;
}

complex complex::sum(complex& x) //sum
{
    return complex(real+x.real, imag+x.imag);
}

void complex::print()              //print
{
  cout << real << " " << imag << endl;
}

void main()
{
complex a(1,2);                        //declare a
a.print();                             //print it
complex b(3,2);                        //declare b
b.print();
b.conjugate();                         //take complex conjugate
b.print();
complex c = a.sum(b);                  //add them
c.print();                             //print result
}
```

Complex Addition by Operator Overloading

It is admittedly a bit inelegant to use a member function like a.sum(b) to
perform complex addition. We would prefer to write

```
c = a + b;
```

and have it understood that the plus sign means perform complex addition.
Fortunately, we can accomplish this in C++ by *overloading* the plus operator.
Overloading an operator amounts to declaring a member function for the complex
class which uses an operator symbol. In this case we declare that the operator "+"
operates on a complex class and returns a complex value:

```
complex operator+ (complex& p);
```

Note the syntax carefully: the keyword "operator" is followed by the operator
symbol "+." It operates on a reference to an instance of a complex class and
returns a complex class instance. The implementation of this function is just as
simple as the sum member function above:

```
complex complex::operator+(complex& p)          //addition
{
 return(complex(real+p.real, imag+p.imag));
}
```

With this overloaded operator as a new member function, our main complex number program allows us to write

```
        c = a + b;
```

and the complete main program is

```
void main()
{
complex a(1,2);                 //declare a
a.print();                      //print it
complex b(3,2);                 //declare b
b.print();
b.conjugate();                  //take complex conjugate
b.print();
complex c = a + b;              //add them
c.print();                      //print result
}
```

Operator Overloading Syntax

When we write an operator member function like

```
complex operator+ (complex& p);
```

we are really dealing with three objects: the current instance, the argument, and the return value. Since this overloaded operator is a *member function*, it must be a member of some instance of the complex class:

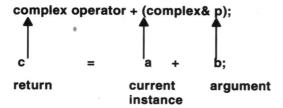

If we write

```
    a + b
```

the current instance is always the left value and the argument the right value. This is equivalent to writing

```
a.operator+ (b)
```

The return value is the result of the operation.

This is somewhat less obvious in the case of the assignment operator (=):

```
a = b;
```

The current instance is *a*, the left operator, the argument is *b*, and the result of the expression

```
(a = b)
```

is the return value. Remember that all C expressions have return values. This is how we can string together assignments on a single line:

```
a = b = c = d;
```

We will see more complete examples of using the assignment operators in Chapter 12 of the Day 2 discussions.

CHAPTER 7

cin and cout

Oh to be wafted away. From this black Aceldama of sorrow,
Where the dust of an earthy today, Is the earth of a dusty tomorrow!
Patience

As we illustrated in Chapter 1, you usually use **cin** and **cout** for terminal input and output in C++. These objects are part of the C++ iostream library, which is provided with all C++ compilers. While there is nothing to prevent your from continuing to use the C **stdio** library functions **printf** and **scanf**, there are significant advantages in utilizing the iostream library.

Foremost among these reasons are that the **cin** and **cout** objects know how to read and write data irrespective of type. They are completely type safe compared to the **stdio** library functions, which can easily cause apparently irrational program behavior. For example, in C there is no checking in **scanf** for either legal pointers or legal types. Thus,

```
        int counter;
        scanf("%d", counter);        //wrong!
and
        scanf("%d", &counter);       //right
```

are both accepted by the compiler and the run time system. Further, you can write

```
        int counter;
        scanf("%f", &counter);       //wrong!
and
        scanf("%d", &counter);       //right
```

and C will blithely convert to a floating point number and store it in the location pointed to be the integer pointer, even if the types are of different numbers of bytes in length.

You can do the same sort of thing with the **printf** function, using the format specifier to print out data of the wrong type:

```
    printf("%s", counter);
```

even though **counter** is not a string at all and does not have enough memory reserved for it.

By contrast, none of these problems occur using the iostream objects, since their member functions are overloaded for all the standard variable types:

```
int counter;
cin  >> counter;                //read in counter
cout << counter << endl;        //print out value
```

As we have been doing right along, we reiterate that input comes from the standard input stream **cin** using the ">>" *extraction operator*,

```
cin >> x >> y;        //read in x and y
```

and output is put into the **cout** output stream using the *insertion operator* "<<". Remember, the data move in the direction the operators point, and the stream name always is written first.

Now, as we just noted, these two operators are overloaded so that the compiler always picks the right one for an input or output operation. For example, you can write

```
int a = 5;
float x = 3.42;

cout << a << x ;
```

and the compiler will select the integer output member function for *a* and the floating point output function for *x*.

This also completely eliminates the formatting *faux pas* of selecting the wrong C formatting string:

```
    float x = 3.42;;
    printf("%d \n", x); /*should be %f */
```

which is likely to lead to "garbage" being printed out mysteriously, since we have asked to print out a **float** in **integer** format.

Characters and Strings

The **cin** object will read in a string up to the first white space (space, tab, or newline) that it finds. Thus, the command

```
    const MAX= 80;
```

```
char instring[MAX];
cin >> instring;
```

will read in the string

```
The Peer and the Peri.
```

only as far as "The." The remainder stays in the input stream. If you want to read in a complete string up to the end of a line, you use the **get** member function:

```
cin.get(instring, MAX);  //read to end of line
```

Like most other member functions, **get** is overloaded, so you can read in single characters as well:

```
char c;
cin.get(c);    //read one character
```

Character Output

In a similar fashion, there is a **put** member function for the **cout** operator which allows you to send single characters to the output stream:

```
char c = 'A';
cout.put(c);         //print 1 character
```

Iostream Member Functions

In addition to the **get** and **put** member functions we introduced above, the iostream classes also have a number of other useful functions shown in Table 1. We can use these functions to check for errors. Suppose we write a simple routine to accept a number and a kind such as "2 Dogs." The simplest code for this is

```
cin >> num >> kind;            //get number and kind
cout <<"Num ="<< num << endl;  //print it out
ccut <<"Kind ="<< kind << endl;
```

If we run this program and enter "2 Dogs," it will indeed print out

```
Num = 2
Kind = Dogs
```

Suppose, however, that someone enters "Dogs 2" instead. The program will print out

```
Num = 4657
Kind = 2
```

This unexpected result arises because the **num** variable is never initialized and no legal value is read in. The **cin** object simply fails on trying to convert "Dogs" to a number and goes on to read the next item for the **kind** variable. Now, if we want to check for the occasional ninny who enters "Dogs 2," we can utilize the **fail** member function as follows:

```
#include <iostream.h>
void main()
{
int num;
char *kind = new char[80];

cout << "enter number and kind:";

do
{
  if (cin.fail())
    {
      cin.clear();         //reset error flags
      cin.ignore(80, '\n');        //ignore rest of current
line
      cout << "Input error, please re-enter number and kind"
<<endl;
    }
  cin >> num >> kind;            //get number and type
  }
while (cin.fail());            //loop until no errors

cout <<"Num ="<< num << endl;
cout <<"Kind ="<< kind << endl;

}
```

Formatting with Manipulators

Input/Output (I/O) *manipulators* are verbs that you can place right in the iostream statements to change the character of the output. These are shown in Table 2. You can use these by including the I/O manipulator header file *iomanip.h*.

```
#include <iomanip.h>

cout << hex << x;    //print out x in hexadecimal
cout << oct << y;    //print out y in octal

//print out 8 characters wide, 3 to right of decimal
cout << setw(8) << setprecision(3) << x;
```

Table 1. Iostream Member Functions	
`int good()`	Returns TRUE if stream is OK
`int fail()`	Returns TRUE if conversion error
`int bad()`	Returns TRUE if unrecoverable error
`void clear()`	Clears error state
`char fill(char c)`	Sets the current fill character
`getline(char *, int n)`	Reads up to n characters to end of line
`ignore(int n, char c);`	Ignores n characters until character c is found
`int precision(int n)`	Sets the current floating point precision
`int width(int n)`	Sets the current floating point width

Table 2. C++ I/O Manipulators	
`dec`	Sets decimal output
`oct`	Sets octal (base-8) output
`hex`	Sets hexadecimal (base-16) output
`endl`	Sends a newline and flushes the buffer
`ends`	Inserts a null (0) character
`setprecision(int)`	Sets the number of digits to the right of the decimal point
`setw(int)`	Sets field width to specified value

References

1. K. Christian, "The C++ Iostream Library," *PC Magazine*, **13**(1), 284, January 11, 1994.

2. S. Teale, *C++ IO Streams,* Addison-Wesley, Reading, MA, 1993.

CHAPTER 8

A SIMPLE EXAMPLE: INCOME TAXES

"Ten years later--Time progresses
Sours your temper--thins your tresses.
Fancy then, her chin relaxes; rates are facts and so are taxes. "
Utopia, Limited

In terms of information hiding, there are few fields more fertile than the U.S. income tax system. You put in income, interest, deductions, and exemptions and a tax payment mysteriously emerges. While the computational method changes every year, there are few changes to the required inputs, and this represents an ideal example of an object-oriented computation.

Let's try to design this program in a top-down fashion. We will need to put in

* salary
* interest
* deductions
* exemptions

So at the outset, we will outline the class as having functions to set these values:

```
class income
{
public:
  income();               //set income with constructor
  set_deductions();       //set deductions
  set_interest();         //set interest
  set_exemptions();       //set exemptions
  get_tax();              //get taxes
};
```

Now, let's decide on the parameters for these member functions. Income, interest, and deductions will be entered as floats and exemptions as integers. Taxes will be returned as floats:

```
class income
{
public:
  void set_deductions(float);
  void set_interest(float);
  void set_exemptions(int);
  float get_tax();
  income(float);
private:
// whatever
};
```

Since there are so many chances for errors in tax computations, we will return an error value along with the taxes in the **get_tax** function:

```
float get_tax(int& err);
```

Now, we can decide what variables we need in the private part of the class. Clearly, these will include salary, deductions, exemptions, and interest. Our class thus finally looks like this:

```
class income
{
public:
  void set_deductions(float);
  void set_interest(float);
  void set_exemptions(int);
  float get_tax(int& err);
  income(float);
private:
  float salary;
  float deductions;
  float interest;
  int exemptions;
};
```

The Constructor

The constructor for this class will set the salary variable to the specified value and set the other members to default values:

```
income::income(float x)
{
  salary =x;            //set the salary
  deductions=0;         //default:no deductions
  interest=0;           //no interest
  exemptions=1;         //and 1 exemption
}
```

The Set Member Functions

The functions for setting the values of deductions, interest, and exemptions are as straightforward as you would expect:

```
void income::set_deductions(float d)   //deductions
{
   deductions = d;
}

void income::set_exemptions(int e)      //exemptions
{
   exemptions = e;
}

void income::set_interest(float i)      //interest
{
   interest = i;
}
```

The Main Program

Now, before we go further, let's see if we have written the right member functions by writing the main program. It should set all these values and return the taxes:

```
void main ()
{
   int err;

   income mine(25500)         //set income into class
   mine.set_interest(400);    //enter interest
   mine.set_exemptions(3);    //set the exemptions
   mine.set_deductions(950);  //and deductions

   //compute and print out the tax
   cout << "your tax= " << mine.get_tax(err) <<endl;
}
```

If we wanted, we could also check for errors:

```
float tax = mine.get_tax(err);
if (err == 0)
   cout << "your tax= " << tax <<endl;
else
   cout << "Tax data error number :" << err <<endl;
```

Computing the Tax

All of our design is independent of the tax laws and computational rules. Thus, we need only rewrite **get_tax** each year to keep our program current. In fact, once we cover inheritance, we may be able to derive new classes each year instead of rewriting them. In this case, for the 1992 tax year, the tax computation is

```
float income::get_tax(int& err)
{
   float tax;
   float gross_income = salary + interest;
   float taxable_income = gross_income -
                          exemptions*2300.00;
if (taxable_income <= 35800)
   {
      tax = 0.15 * taxable_income;
   }
if((taxable_income > 35800) && (taxable_income <= 86500))
   {
      tax = 5370 + 0.28 * (taxable_income - 35800);
   }
if (taxable_income > 86500)
   {
      tax = 19566 + 0.31 * (taxable_income - 86500);
   }
err = 0;                 //no errors in this example
return(tax);
}
```

where we do not carry out any error checking.

Constructor With Default Arguments

We could also specify a single constructor which sets all four parameters -- *salary*, *deductions*, *interest*, and *exemptions*, and which sets default values for those which are not specified:

```
income::income(float x, float deduct=0.0,
               float inter=0.0, int exempt=1 )
{
   salary  =x;
   deductions = deduct;
   interest = inter;
   exemptions = exempt;
}
```

Then, our main program simply becomes

```
void main ()
{
int err;

income mine(25500, 950, 400, 3);

cout << "your tax= " << mine.get_tax(err) <<endl;
}
```

We could also write

```
income mine(25500);
```

and have the default values for the other three parameters take effect. This method is less readable, however, because the order of the parameters is not obvious.

Error Checking in the Tax Object

In order to complete this example, we really should check for common errors. We first define the error return codes as a series of enumerated symbols:

```
enum Taxerr {NONE, NEG_EXMPT, TOOBIG_EXMPT,
             NEG_DEDUCT, NEG_INT, NEG_INCOME};
```

Then we include a private function for checking the data integrity:

```
class income {
public:
  void set_deductions(float);
  void set_interest(float);
  void set_exemptions(int);
  float get_tax(int& err);
  income(float);
private:
  float salary;
  float deductions;
  float interest;
  int exemptions;
  Taxerr check_data();
};
```

Such a function would return a variable of type **Taxerr** and contain the following tests:

```
Taxerr income::check_data()
{
Taxerr errval = NONE;      //default= no error
if (exemptions < 0)        //exmptions < 0
   errval = NEG_EXMPT;
if (exemptions > 10)       //too many exemptions
   errval = TOOBIG_EXMPT;
if (deductions < 0  )      //deductions < 0
   errval = NEG_DEDUCT;
if (interest < 0)          //interest < 0
   errval = NEG_INT;
if (salary < 0)            //salary < 0
   errval = NEG_INCOME;

return errval;             //return error value
}
```

Finally, we incorporate that test in our tax computation function:

```
float income::get_tax(int& err) {
  float tax = 0;                   //initialize tax to 0
  err = check_data();              //check for errors
  if (err == NONE)        //if no errors do computation
  {
  float gross_income = salary + interest;
  float taxable_income = gross_income -
                    exemptions*2300.00;
  if (taxable_income <=35800) {
    tax = 0.15*taxable_income;
  }
  if ((taxable_income >35800)
          &&(taxable_income <= 86500)) {
    tax = 5370 + 0.28*(taxable_income - 35800);
  }
  if (taxable_income >86500) {
    tax = 19566 + 0.31*(taxable_income - 86500);
  }
}
return(tax); //and err is set to NONE or Taxerr value
}
```

CHAPTER 9

A SIMPLE STRING CLASS

I'll tell you how we'll manage it. Let me marry Yum-Yum tomorrow, and in a month you may behead me
No, no. I draw the line at Yum-Yum.
Very good. If you can draw the line [preparing rope] so can I.
The Mikado

Suppose that we want to build a class for manipulating strings. We find that neither C nor C++ provide any easy way to do this. Strings are treated as null-terminated arrays of **char** and have no operations which work directly on them. The string class provides an ideal example of a class which requires you to manipulate memory as well as handle the character data itself.

In the string class, we will want to

- store and fetch string data
- determine the string length
- convert the string to uppercase
- concatenate strings

So, in our first outline of a string class, we might write

```
class string
{
 public:
    string(char *);        //constructor
    ~string();             //destructor
    int Len();             //length function
    void uppercase();      //convert to uppercase
    void print();          //print string
    //???
 private:
    //???
};
```

To construct the private members of the class, we recognize that we will at least need an array of **char**. Further, we might as well keep the length separately for convenience and computing efficiency, since recomputing it each time is a waste of resources:

```
class string
{
 public:
    string(char *);          //constructor
    ~string();               //destructor
    int Len();               //length function
    void uppercase();        //convert to uppercase
    void print();            //print string
 private:
    char *s;                 //string pointer
    int size;                //string length
};
```

Concatenating Strings

It would be convenient to implement the string concatenation operator with the plus sign, as is done in BASIC. This would complete our string class with

```
class string
{
 public:
    string(char *);                    //constructor
    ~string();                         //destructor
    int Len();                         //length function
    void uppercase();                  //convert to uppercase
    void print();                      //print string
    string operator+ (string& );  //concatenate
 private:
    char *s;                           //string pointer
    int size;                          //string length
};
```

Then we can write statements like

```
    c = a + b;
```

where all three are strings.

Note that we declare the plus operator to have an argument of **string&**, meaning that a *pointer* to a string is passed, rather than a copy of the string itself.

The String Constructor

The string constructor is much like the ones we have written earlier in this book. It actually has to do some work:
- computing the string length and storing it
- reserving memory for the string

- copying the string into the memory

```
string::string(char *c)          //constructor
{
    size = strlen(c);            //compute size
    s = new char[size + 1];      //acquire memory
    strcpy(s, c);                //copy the string
}
```

Again, we remind you that you must allocate one extra byte for the string's null terminator.

The Destructor

Similarly, the string destructor must release that memory so it isn't lost when that instance of the string class is no longer needed:

```
string::~string()          //destructor
{
    delete s;          //deallocate memory
}
```

The Basic Member Functions

These member functions are very simple:
- return the length
- convert to uppercase
- print out string

and they require little explanation:

```
int string::Len()          //return the string length
{
    return size;          //which is stored internally
}
//--------------------------------------------
void string::uppercase()  //convert to uppercase
{
    strupr(s);            //just call library function
}
//--------------------------------------------
void string::print()      //print out the string
{
    cout << s <<endl;      //including newline
}
```

We note that the **strupr** function is not available in all Unix systems but is part of most PC-based compilers. Further, the **print** function prints out the string followed by a newline character: this may not always be desirable, but it is useful in this simple example.

The String Concatenation Operator

The concatenation operator takes two existing strings and combines them end to end. To do this inside our string class, we need to

- compute the total string length
- create memory space for the combined string
- copy the first string into it
- concatenate the second string to it

We do this in the following function:

```
string string::operator+ (string& x)    //concatenation
{
    char *tmp;
    int k = size + x.Len();       //get total size
    tmp = new char[k + 1];        //reserve space
    strcpy(tmp, s);               //copy string in
    strcat(tmp, x.s);
    return string(tmp);           //return new string
}
```

The Calling Program

Now that we have the base functions all written, we can easily write a calling program to use them:

```
void main()
{
    string a("abcd");        //create a string
    a.print();               //print it out
    string b("efgh");        //create a 2nd string
    string c = a + b;        //concatenate them
    c.uppercase();           //convert to oppercase
    c.print();               //and print out result
}
```

Now, this program works exactly as we have shown it above. However, it works mainly by luck. It turns out that there is still a major hole to be plugged. The problem also exists in our previous complex number example and is obvious in the above code--can you spot it?

We will take up these and related issues in the Day 2 section of the book. For now, take a look at the problems that follow and work out solutions for all of them before you go on.

Exercises to Gain Experience

1. Write a program to print out your name using the **iostream** member functions.

2. Each number in a Fibonacci series is the sum of the previous two terms of the series: 1,1,2,3,5,8.... Write a C++ program to print out the first 20 terms of the Fibonacci series.

3. Write a program to read in 10 numbers and sort them into ascending order. Can you use classes in any useful way here?

4. Create a thermometer class which measures temperature using either a random number generator function or keyboard input. Create member functions to print out the temperature in Fahrenheit or Celsius. How about Kelvin? Rankine?

5. Create classes for square and circle. Create member functions to compute and print their area.

6. Create a line class which contains two point class coordinates. Write a program to determine if line 2 will intersect line 1.

DAY 2

REVIEW

In our first day's discussion, we went over the improvements that have been made between C and C++ and showed how the **class** is just a more complete sort of structure. We introduced constructors and destructors and showed how to perform input and output using the stream functions **cin** and **cout**. Then we built several examples: complex numbers, taxes, and a string class and left you with some assignments to work out.

In this second day's discussion, we will go over some of the homework problems, discuss copy constructors and assignment operators, complete the discussion of inheritance we began in Chapter 6, and do an object-oriented design exercise.

As before, we suggest that you read this section and work the exercises before going on to the Day 3 discussion.

CHAPTER 10

WRITING A FIBONACCI SERIES

About binomial theorem I'm teeming with a lot of news--
With many cheerful facts about the square of the hypotenuse.
The Pirates of Penzance

One of the exercises for Day 1 was to write a program containing a class which generated a Fibonacci series. In this chapter we will go over how you can create a Fibonacci object which returns the next element in the series each time it is called.

To review, each item in the Fibonacci series is always the sum of the two previous elements:

1, 1, 2, 3, 5, 8, 13, ...

Let us recast this slightly as

(0), 1, 1, 2, 3, 5, 8, 13 ...

where we start with a previous value of zero and a current value of 1. From the outset we can always return the current value without creating a special beginning case.

Now we will create a class **Fibo**, which is initialized by the constructor and which has a single member function **nextnum** which returns the next number in the series:

```
class Fibo
{
public:
   float nextnum();         //get next in series
   Fibo();                  //constructor
private: //???
};
```

The Calling Program

We just want to print out 10 values, including their index. We could do this easily with the following:

```
void main()
{
 Fibo f1;                  //Fibonacci class
 int i;
 for (i =1; i <= 10; i++)
   {
     cout << i <<" " << f1.nextnum() << endl;
   }
}
```

The Private Members

To compute the series, a Fibonacci object will have to have "memory," keeping the last and current values at all times. This is one of the places where an object-oriented approach has a great advantage, that is, each object can contain persistent values:

```
class fibo {

public:
   float nextnum();   //function to get next value
   fibo();
private:
   float thisval;     //current value
   float nextval;     //next value to be returned
   };
```

Then, recognizing that we will always return the value in **thisval**, we can set up a constructor for the class as

```
fibo::fibo()           //constructor initializes internals
  {
    thisval =0;        //initialize current
    nextval =1;        //and next values
  }
```

Computing the Series

Now, with this in place, we can easily write our member function **nextnum**:

```
float fibo::nextnum()
{
 float next =thisval + nextval;//compute new value
 thisval = nextval;        //copy next to current
 nextval = next;           //copy new to next value
 return thisval;           //return current value
```

```
}
```

The Complete Fibo Program

Now we can see that the complete program will be

```cpp
#include <iostream.h>
/*----------- Fibonacci series printout routine----------*/
class fibo {

public:
  float nextnum();   //function to get next value
  fibo();
private:
  float thisval;     //current value
  float nextval;
  };
fibo::fibo()               //constructor initializes internals
  {
  thisval =0;       //initialize current
  nextval =1;       //and next values
  }
float fibo::nextnum()
{
  float next =thisval + nextval;  //compute new value
  thisval = nextval;      //copy next to current
  nextval = next;         //copy new to next value
  return thisval;         //return current value
  }
void main()
{
  fibo f1;                // one instance of fibo
  int i;
  for (i=1; i <= 10; i++)          //print out 10 values
  {
    cout << i <<" "<<f1.nextnum()<< endl;
  }
}
```

which prints out the values

1, 1, 2, 3, 5, 8, 13, 21, 34, 55

CHAPTER 11

THE COPY CONSTRUCTOR

To you I give my heart so rich.
To which?
I do not care
Iolanthe

Recall, at the end of Day 1, we noted that the string class program we developed was actually incomplete and worked only by good fortune. The calling program in this example was

```
//---main program for illustrating string class---
void main()
{
string a("abcd");              //create a string
a.print();                     //print
string b("efgh");              //create b
ate b string string c = a + b ;  //concatenate
c.uppercase();                 //convert to uppercase
c.print();                     //print again
}
```

The Copy Constructor

In order to appreciate the problem illustrated above, we will now take up the copy constructor. C++ allows you to create an instance of a class and copy all the values from one object to another in a single statement. For the class **lrectangle**, we can create and copy values into the new object as follows:

```
lrectangle ar(12,14);   //create new object ar
lrectangle br = ar;     //copy values into br
lrectangle br(ar);      //alternate syntax for copying
```

In either case, the copy statements perform a member-by-member copy of all the members of one object into the new one.

Now, you might not always want to copy every member from one object to another without change, since in some cases there may be pointer values within an object that should not be blithely copied. For such cases, C++ provides a *copy constructor* which allows you to create a new object by copying and modifying those members which should not be copied indiscriminately.

Suppose we have a special rectangle class **lrectangle** which contains a pointer to allow us to make a linked list of rectangles. You probably would not link together a list of objects such that two had the same pointer and we would indeed want to interfere in the copying process:

```
class lrectangle
{
 private:
    float height, width;
    int xpos, ypos;
    lrectangle *link;
public:
    ....
};
```

In this case, we could create a copy constructor as part of the public class interface. The copy constructor comes into play if either of the above copying syntaxes are used:

```
class lrectangle
{
 private:
   float height, width;
   int xpos, ypos;
   lrectangle *link;
public:
    lrectangle(float h, float w);        //constructor
    lrectangle(lrectangle &a);           //copy constructor
    ....
};
```

The implementation of the copy constructor function is

```
lrectangle::lrectangle(lrectangle &a)
{
 height = a.height;        //copy height and width
 width = a.width;
 xpos= a.xpos;             //copy x and y position
 ypos = a.ypos;
 link =0;                  //and set pointer to 0
}
```

We don't really know in general what we would do with the pointer *link,* so in this case, we just set it to zero. This is preferable to allowing a copy of a pointer from the other object to remain, since if the pointer is deleted in one instance, the pointer in the other instance will become invalid.

Now regardless of which syntax you use for copying into a new instance

```
lrectangle br = ar;       //copy into new one
```

```
    //or
lrectangle br(ar);         //copy this way
```

the copy constructor will be called.

Remember, you need to create a copy constructor every time a class contains pointers or other elements you don't want to replicate exactly.

Overloading the Assignment Operator

While the copy constructor copies data into a new instance, the assignment operator copies the members of a class into another *already existing* instance. For example, below, we declare **ar** and **br** to be instances of the class **lrectangle** and then later copy the current values of **ar** into **br**:

```
lrectangle ar(10, 20);   // declare instance ar
lrectangle br(0,0);      // and br
    // ;                  //Then, later...
br = ar;                  //assign br values to ar
```

You can define a special action for assignment statements by redefining the equals operator. The actual code inside the member function is much the same:

```
lrectangle& lrectangle::operator = (lrectangle &a)
{
   height = a.height; //copy values
   width= a.width;
   xpos = a.xpos;
   ypos = a.ypos;
   link = 0;       //zero pointer
}
```

Is This Trick Really Necessary?

Copy constructors and assignment operators end up being important in programs, and in the most surprising ways, because many program statements can reduce to one or the other. One way to find out if you need to include copy constructors and assignment operators is to include the prototypes for these member functions in the *private* section of the class. You don't actually have to write these member functions: just include the prototypes. Then if you write code that calls them inadvertently, the compiler will flag these statements as errors.

For example, in the **string** class below we include these prototypes:

```
class string
{
   private:
      char *s;               //string pointer
      int size;              //and length are private
```

```
    string(string &);        //protective copy constructor
    void operator = (string &);//protective operator

  public:
    string(char *);              //constructor
    ~string();                   //destructor
    int  Len() ;                 //return length
    void uppercase();            //convert to uppercase
    void print();
    string operator+(string& ); //concatenate
};
```

Finding Inadvertent Bugs

Now, let's reconsider the string class we wrote at the end of Day 1. If we add these two private member functions and compile the program

```
void main()
{
 string a("abcd");    //create a string
 a.print();           //print
 string b("efgh");    //create b string
 string c = a + b ;   //concatenate
 c.uppercase();       //convert to uppercase
 c.print();           //print again
}
```

we will get the error message from Borland C++ for Windows similar to the one below :

```
Linker Error:
 Undefined symbol string::string(string near&)
```

This occurs because the function prototype for the copy constructor appears in the private section, but no function is ever provided. Other C++ compilers also flag this as a link error, noting that the copy constructor function was not defined.

Clearly, then, we must actually write a copy constructor for the string class. Remember that the copy constructor creates a new object,

```
 string::string(string& x)
{
 char *tmp;                  //create a new one
 size =  x.Len();            //compute size
 tmp = new char[size + 1];   //make room for it
 strcpy(tmp, x.s);           //copy 1st string
 s = tmp;
 }
```

while the assignment operator works on an already valid object,

```
void string::operator=(string& x)
  {                          //assignment operator redefined
```

```
char *tmp;                    //create a new one
size =  x.Len();              //compute combined size
tmp = new char[size + 1];     //make room for it
strcpy(tmp, x.s);             //copy 1st string
delete s;                     //remove old string
s = tmp;                      //put in new one
}
```

Note that these two routines are almost the same:
- Both allocate memory for a new string of the same length.
- Both copy the **char** array into it.
- Both change the **char** pointer to point to the new array.

The difference is that the assignment operator works on an already valid object and must release previously assigned string memory, while the copy constructor has no previously assigned memory to delete, since it is creating a new instance of the class as it copies.

Reusing Code

Now, with one small change, we could use much of the code over again. Let us write the private function **copystring**. This function does the same thing as the assignment operator: it allocates new memory, copies and deletes:

```
class string {
  private:
    char *s;               //string pointer
    int size;           //and length are private
    void copystring(string& );

  public:
    string(char *);                //constructor
    ~string();                     //destructor
    int  Len() ;                   //return length
    void uppercase();              //convert to uppercase
    void print();
    string operator+(string& );  //concatenate
    void operator = (string &); //assignment operator
    string(string &);            //copy constructor
    };
void string::copystring(string& x)
{
  char *tmp;                    //create a new one
  size = x.Len();               //compute combined size
  tmp = new char[size + 1];     //make room for it
  strcpy(tmp, x.s);             //copy 1st string
  delete s;              //delete old
  s = tmp;
}
```

Then we can write our assignment operator as

```
// assignment operator (=)
void string::operator=(string& x) //assignment operator
{
    copystring(x);
}
```

We can use this same code for the copy constructor if we provide a string for it to delete. So we simply add the following to allocate 1 byte:

```
//copy constructor
string::string(string& x)
{
 s = new char [1];         //allocate 1 byte
 copystring(x);
}
```

Now we have used the same code twice and have written two public functions which call a private member function. We'll see in the next chapter how we can protect such programs from unwarranted intrusions.

Summary

In summary, the copy constructor and overloaded assignment operator should be used whenever a class contains pointers or other values which should not be copied directly into a new object. You should put a dummy for each of these in the private section of each new class so that if you inadvertently call one of these functions, the compiler will warn you.

CHAPTER 12

BULLETPROOFING YOUR PROGRAMS

With an ounce or two of lead, I despatched him through the head.
Like a stone I saw him sinking. I should say a lump of lead.
The Yeoman of the Guard

Now that we have begun to write some fairly interesting C++ programs, you probably would like to have all the help you can get in avoiding programming errors. In this chapter, we will discuss several techniques for professionalizing and "bulletproofing" your programs.

Naming Your Classes

The **string** class we created in the previous chapter is somewhat naively named. Nearly everyone writes some sort of a string class and often names it **string**. Further, any number of commercially available and shareware class libraries contain string classes. Thus, we strongly suggest that your personalize your class names to avoid naming conflicts with other libraries you may use.

One way to do this is by adding your initials or your company or project's name to the beginning of the class name. In this case, we will name the "professional" version of our string class **clString** and expand the error protection using the **const** modifier.

The const Modifier

As we have seen, it is common to pass an object into member functions by reference:

```
void clString::operator=(clString& x)
```

We do this primarily for computational efficiency: if we don't pass the argument in by reference, the entire contents of the structure that makes up the class is copied onto the stack before the function is called. If we pass the object by reference, only the address of the instance is passed to the function.

However, while this may be more efficient in terms of computing cycles consumed, it does leave us open to the danger of changing the contents of this object unintentionally. C++ provides us with protection against accidentally changing these variables with the **const** operator:

```
void clString::operator=(const clString& x)
```

This operator indicates that while the string *x* is passed to the operator member function by reference, that function may not change any of its values.

So, consider the string copy constructor and assignment operator we developed in the previous chapter. By simply prefixing the arguments with **const**, we prevent accidental change to the variable passed in:

```
//assignment operator redefined
void clString::operator=(const clString& x)
{
    copystring(x);
}

//copy constructor
clString::clString(const clString& x)
{
  s = new char[1];
  copystring(x);
}
```

Since the copy constructor and assignment operator member functions both call **copystring**, you must also specify that its argument is protected with the **const** modifier:

```
void clString::copystring(const clString& x)
{
  char *tmp;                //create a new one
  size =  x.Len();          //compute combined size
  tmp = new char[size + 1];     //make room for it
  strcpy(tmp, s);           //copy 1st string
  delete s;                 //delete old string
  s = tmp                   //copy in new pointer;
}
```

Extending const to Called Member Functions

Of course, if we say that the copy constructor and assignment operator have constant pointers as arguments, we have to continue this all the way down the chain of any functions these routines call as well. The **copystring** function calls the member function **Len**, and so, it too must be declared not to change any member of its class. For cases where the member function has no arguments, C++ provides the following somewhat peculiar syntax:

```
int clString::Len() const { //return string length
   return size;
}
```

Note the unusual placement of the **const** keyword: after the function name and before the opening brace of the member function.

Getting the String Pointer

While there are advantages to having your own string class, because standard C string functions are so awkward to use, some C library functions require the use of null-terminated strings. Thus our professional grade string class also needs a function to return a standard C string pointer. Thus, we will add a **GetStr** function:

```
char * clString::GetStr() const
{
return s;
}
```

which returns the string pointer for use in C functions such as **fopen**. Note that this new member function also requires the **const** modifier.

Protecting from Multiple Definitions

When you develop a complete, useful class, you usually put the class definition in an include file (*clstring.h*) so that you can reference the class in each module you develop. Since additional classes then require the *clstring.h* header file to define your class, it does not take long before you have created a header file which includes *clstring.h* and which itself is included in a program module which also includes *clstring.h*.

In such cases, the compiler will see the **clstring** class defined twice, once inside the header file and again inside the main program which includes that header file. To prevent this apparent duplicate definition of types, it is common to include an **#ifndef** declaration surrounding each include file so that it is only included once. For example, we might surround the include file statements with

```
#ifndef CL_STRING
   #define CL_STRING
   //include file statements
#endif
```

These declarations cause the include file statements to be included once, but since the variable CL_STRING is then defined, these statements are skipped each additional time they are encountered.

Thus, our final **clString** class definition looks like this:

```
#ifndef CL_STRING
#define CL_STRING
class clString {
  public:
    clString(char *);              //constructor
    ~clString();                   //destructor
    int  Len() const;              //return length
    void uppercase();              //convert to uppercase
    clString operator+(const clString& ) const; //concat
    void operator= (const clString&);
    clString(const clString&);
    char *GetStr() const       //get string
private:
    char *s;               //string pointer
    int size;              //and length are private
    void copystring(const clString&);
};
#endif
```

Summary

In summary, you should pass any class instance or other structure to member functions by *reference* rather than by value to save unnecessary recopying of structures. Then, you should use the **const** modifier to prevent such arguments from being inadvertently modified within the function. Finally, you should utilize **#ifndef** - **#endif** pairs using some convenient and otherwise unused variable name to bracket all class header files.

CHAPTER 13

INHERITANCE

My good sir, if you can't disinherit your own unborn son, whose unborn son can you disinherit?
Ruddigore

By now you have seen how C++ simplifies many aspects of C programming: References can be used instead of pointers in function calls, inline functions can replace macros, and you can easily define your own new data types using classes. The class mechanism really starts to open a new perspective in developing programs that more closely map to the parts of your applications. In this chapter, we'll develop the notion of deriving new data types from existing ones. The real power of C++ as an object-oriented language will become apparent.

Inheritance is defined as a means for new classes to acquire, access, and use existing methods and data from other classes. It is the feature that enables the true power of object-oriented programming. When a class inherits from another class, there are three benefits:

1. You can reuse the methods and data of the existing class.

2. You can extend the existing class by adding new data members and new methods.

3. You can modify the existing class by overriding its methods with your own implementations.

We will explore the reuse, extensibility, and modification of classes next. First, we need some terminology about the relationships between existing classes and new classes that inherit from them. The terms vary, depending on what object-oriented language is being discussed. In C++, an existing class which serves as the base, or starting point, from which other classes inherit is called a *Base Class*. A class which inherits from a base class is called a *Derived Class*. Other ways to refer to these types are parent and child or superclass and subclass. Base and derived class are preferred in C++ and are what we will use in this book.

Reusing and Extending Objects

To see how derived classes reuse the data and methods of the base class from which they inherit, consider the following class describing a hypothetical camera object:

```
// a base class
class Camera
{

public:
    void TakePicture();    // snaps a picture
    void AdvanceFilm();    // increments the
                           // picture number

private:
    int PictureNumber;    // holds current film position

};
```

We can use this as a starting point, or base class, and derive a new class:

```
// a derived class
class GoodCamera : public Camera
{

public:
    void SetExposure(int f, int e);

private:
    int Fstop;           // aperture setting
    int ExposureTime;    // length of exposure

};
```

Our **GoodCamera** class has some variables that are not in the camera base class, and these variables can be initialized with a new method, **SetExposure()**. The only difference from the normal class declaration syntax for **GoodCamera** is the **public Camera** declaration following the colon. This signifies that **GoodCamera** is a derived class, and it inherits from a base class named **Camera**. The significance of the **public** keyword in declaring new classes will be discussed later.

We could have accomplished the same thing without inheritance by declaring our derived class as follows, copying the code for the **TakePicture()** and **AdvanceFilm()** methods from the code for **Camera**:

```
// an alternate definition without inheritance
class GoodCamera
{
```

```
public:
    void TakePicture();      // snaps a picture
    void AdvanceFilm();      // increments the
                             // picture number
    void SetExposure(int f, int e);
private:
    int PictureNumber;       // holds current film position
    int Fstop;               // aperture setting
    int ExposureTime;        // length of exposure
};
```

This implementation of **GoodCamera** is a perfectly good class, but it requires two copies of the same code and data: one copy for objects of type **Camera** and one copy for objects of type **GoodCamera**. By contrast, we get effectively the same class by inheriting the **Camera** class, using our first definition of **GoodCamera**. And we no longer have to copy the methods or data from the base class. **GoodCamera** is reusing the base class code that has already been written (and presumably debugged). The author of the **GoodCamera** class can therefore concentrate on the implementation of the new features of the data type, without worrying about breaking either the code inside **Camera** or any code which currently uses camera objects.

Furthermore, our derived class has extended the notion of the base class to include new variables and new methods. Not only have we reused the **Camera** code, we added additional code without changing anything in the original implementation! How often have you done that in C?

Better still, the programmer does not even need access to the source code of the base class to write a derived class. The only thing required is the base class declaration, which can be in a header file. The actual base class code [**Camera::TakePicture()**, **Camera::AdvanceFilm()**, etc.] can reside in an object module or library.

Once defined, derived classes are declared and used just as other classes or data types. And we can use a derived class anywhere its base class can be legally used. Thus, any code you write to manipulate a base class will also work with any class derived from the base. We'll see an example of this later. For now, we can declare instances of the camera objects:

```
Camera a110Camera;
GoodCamera a35mmCamera;
```

With these declarations, we can call any of the methods defined for these classes. So **a110Camera** can call **TakePicture()** and **AdvanceFilm()**, while

a35mmCamera can call both of these methods in addition to calling **SetExposure()**:

```
a110Camera.TakePicture();
a110Camera.AdvanceFilm();

a35mmCamera.SetExposure(8, 100);
a35mmCamera.TakePicture();
a35mmCamera.AdvanceFilm();
```

However, **a110Camera** cannot access any methods or data of classes that are derived from **Camera**. So the statement **a110Camera.SetExposure(8, 100)** would be flagged as a compile error. Similarly, the **Fstop** and **ExposureTime** variables can only be accessed by objects of type **GoodCamera**.

In general, base classes cannot use methods or data defined in classes derived from the base, but derived classes can do anything their base classes can do. Later on, we will see that this is not exactly true, because we can control what actually gets inherited from a base class, and we can defer method resolution until the program is actually running.

Building a Class Hierarchy

Derived classes are special cases of base classes. But a derived class can also serve as a base class for new classes. For example, here is a new class which inherits from **GoodCamera**:

```
class BetterCamera : public GoodCamera
{
public:
    void SetFocus(int f);

private:
    int FocusSetting;    // focus distance (in feet)

};
```

This new class inherits all the functionality of **GoodCamera**, which already includes the functionality of **Camera**. Thus, the author of **BetterCamera** need only implement the **SetFocus()** function. Programs can then use the class as if it contained all the methods and data of the other two base classes:

```
BetterCamera proCamera;

// call BetterCamera methods
proCamera.SetFocus(200);

// also call GoodCamera methods
```

```
proCamera.SetExposure(8, 100);

// and call Camera methods too
proCamera.TakePicture();
proCamera.AdvanceFilm();
```

It is not necessary to specify both base classes in the declaration of **BetterCamera**. **GoodCamera** already inherits from **Camera**, so you only have to declare one level of inheritance. There is also no limit on the depth of inheritance allowed in C++, so you can carry the inheritance concept as far as you want within the limits of your compiler.

It is also possible that a class can be a base class for more than one derived class. Thus, we can define a new class called **AutoCamera** that also uses **GoodCamera** as a base class:

```
class AutoCamera : public GoodCamera
{

public:
    void AutoExpose();    // set exposure automatically

};
```

You can build up a hierarchy, or taxonomy, of classes very easily. We have effectively constructed the following camera model class hierarchy in the discussion above:

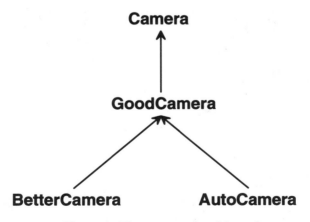

Figure 1. The camera class hierarchy

It is customary when drawing class hierarchies to draw arrows which point from a derived class to its base class. Hierarchy diagrams are useful because you can tell at a glance what classes depend on others and therefore what functionality a particular class has.

For example, by referring to Figure 1, it is clear that **BetterCamera** and **AutoCamera** are both **GoodCamera** objects. **GoodCamera** is also a **Camera** object, so all classes in the diagram are valid **Camera** objects. Furthermore, **BetterCamera** and **AutoCamera** objects can only call their own methods or methods in their common base class, **GoodCamera**, or **GoodCamera**'s base class, **Camera**. **BetterCamera** objects cannot call the **AutoCamera::AutoExpose()** method, nor can **AutoCamera** objects call the **BetterCamera::SetFocus()** method.

Modifying Class Behavior

The camera example demonstrates code reuse and extensibility through inheritance. What about modification of existing class behavior? For example, suppose we want to define a new **TakePicture()** method in the **AutoCamera** class. **AutoCamera** already inherits a **TakePicture()** method from **Camera**, but we want the implementation of **TakePicture()** for an automatic camera to make a call to **AutoExpose()** first:

```
class Camera
{

public:
    void TakePicture();     // snaps a picture
    void AdvanceFilm();     // increments the
                            // picture number

private:
    int PictureNumber;      // holds current film position

};


class AutoCamera : public GoodCamera
{

public:
    void TakePicture();     // replaces the Camera method
    void AutoExpose();

};
```

We are simply redefining, or *overloading*, the **TakePicture()** method in **AutoCamera**. Now we can implement the overloaded method as follows:

```
void AutoCamera::TakePicture()
{
    AutoExpose();    // set exposure automatically

    // ... and take the picture
}
```

And we can write code that uses both **TakePicture()** methods:

```
Camera foolproof;
AutoCamera novice;

// this calls the TakePicture() method in
// the Camera class
foolproof.TakePicture();

// this calls the TakePicture() method in
// the AutoCamera class
novice.TakePicture();
```

The compiler was able to distinguish which method to call based on the type of object. As **novice** is an **AutoCamera** object, the **AutoCamera::TakePicture()** method is called. Similarly, **foolproof** is a **Camera** object, so the **Camera::TakePicture()** method is called. These two camera types were identified when the source code was compiled. The determination of which method to call at compile time is termed *static binding*, *early binding*, or *compile time resolution*.

What happens in a more complicated example where we define a function which takes a **Camera** object as an argument? Inside our function, we call the **TakePicture()** method for whatever type of object that is passed as an argument:

```
// simple function that is not part of a class - the
// argument to this function is a reference to any type
// of Camera object
void Controller(Camera& c)
{
    // take a picture with this camera object
    c.TakePicture();
}
```

Note that we can use this function on any type of **Camera** object. Any derived classes of the base class **Camera** represent valid objects that can be passed to the **Controller()** function. The derived classes are simply specialized types of the base class. We will therefore use the above function on both **Camera** and **AutoCamera** objects:

```
Camera foolproof;
```

```
AutoCamera novice;

// this will result in calling
// the Camera::TakePicture() method
Controller(foolproof);

// surprise!  this will also call
// the Camera::TakePicture() method
Controller(novice);
```

Why didn't **Controller()** call the **AutoCamera::TakePicture()** function defined for **novice**? Note that our function takes a reference to any valid camera object as the input argument, and both **foolproof** and **novice** are valid **Camera** objects. However, there is no way for the compiler to know that **c** might represent an **AutoCamera** object when the **Controller()** function is compiled. We must tell the compiler that the method resolution for TakePicture() should take place at run time, not compile time.

To allow *run time resolution*, *late binding*, or *dynamic binding*, C++ introduces the **virtual** keyword. If we simply add this keyword to our definition of **TakePicture()** in our **Camera** class declaration, the determination of which overloaded method to call will be determined at run time:

```
class Camera
{

public:
    virtual void TakePicture();   // snaps a picture
    void AdvanceFilm();           // increments the
                                  // picture number

private:
    int PictureNumber;    // holds current film position

};
```

With this new declaration, the **Controller()** function will call the appropriate **TakePicture()** method when our example code is run. The **virtual** keyword in the class declaration informs the compiler that it should look up which **TakePicture()** class method to call based on the actual data type passed to **Controller()**.

C doesn't have a built-in mechanism for late binding. If we had programmed **Controller()** in C, we would probably have added a parameter denoting the type of object passed in (e.g., 0 for **Camera** and 1 for **AutoCamera**). Then a switch statement would call the appropriate function, depending on the object type:

```
// a C solution
void Controller(void *c, int type)
{
    switch (type)
```

```
{
    case 0:     // cast c to a Camera object
                // and call the TakePicture()
                // method for Camera
    {
        Camera *t1 = (Camera *)c;
        t1->TakePicture();
    }
    break;

    case 1:     // cast c to an AutoCamera
                // object and call the
                // TakePicture method for
                // AutoCamera
    {
        AutoCamera *t2 = (AutoCamera *)c;
        t2->TakePicture();
    }
    break;

    default:    // error!  unrecognized type
    }
}
```

The C implementation is not as clean, requires more arguments, must do additional error checking, and is harder to modify and maintain. By contrast, all we had to do in C++ was add the **virtual** keyword to the method in the class declaration.

Summary

We have introduced the concept of inheritance for code reuse, extensibility, and modification. We learned the basic terminology and syntax for building class hierarchies and how to use the **virtual** keyword to implement dynamic binding.

CHAPTER 14

ENCAPSULATION OF METHODS AND DATA

We'll go down to Posterity renowned
As the First Sovereign in Christendom
Who registered his Crown and Country under
The Joint Stock Company's Act of Sixty-Two.
Utopia, Limited

In the last chapter, we showed a number of examples illustrating how derived classes can call methods in base classes. Although some of the classes contained private data, we intentionally omitted the issue of how to access these data. Earlier, we introduced the notion of private data that encapsulate the state of an object. That raises the question of how derived classes can get to the data in their base classes.

Private data are only accessible to objects of that specific class. Derived classes therefore cannot access the private data of a base class. We could declare those variables public if we wanted derived classes to get access to the variables. But that violates the principle of encapsulation: public access means that any object or function can get to the data. It would be easy for other objects or functions to change the data and put the object into an inconsistent state (e.g., free memory, place invalid values into variables, etc.).

Protected Members

C++ uses a new access specifier keyword, **protected**, to solve this problem. Declaring methods and variables as protected means that functions or objects outside the class cannot access them -- they are effectively private. However, derived classes are granted access to protected members of their base classes.

Consider the camera example again. We will define the derived class **AutoWindCamera** from the **Camera** base class:

```
class Camera
```

```
{
public:
    virtual void TakePicture();    // snaps a picture
    void AdvanceFilm();            // increments the
                                   // picture number

private:
    int PictureNumber;    // holds current film position

};
// a derived class
class AutoWindCamera : public Camera
{

public:
    void TakePicture();    // overloaded method

};
```

Now we define the implementation of **TakePicture()** for an **AutoWindCamera** object. The method should first call the base class **TakePicture()** method. Then the private variable **PictureNumber** should be incremented by 1 to emulate a self-advancing film camera attachment:

```
void AutoWindCamera::TakePicture()
{
    // use scope resolution operator to call
    // the base class TakePicture() function
    Camera::TakePicture();

    PictureNumber += 1;    // ERROR! PictureNumber is
                           // private in Camera class
}
```

The first statement in this method calls the **TakePicture()** method defined in the base class. The scope resolution operator (::) allows us to specify which class a method is in. As written, the second statement generates a compile error, because **PictureNumber** is a private variable in **Camera**, so **AutoWindCamera** objects cannot access the variable. However, we can simply change the access specifier in **Camera** from **private** to **protected**, and the **AutoWindCamera** implementation will compile correctly:

```
class Camera
{

public:
    virtual void TakePicture();    // snaps a picture
    void AdvanceFilm();            // increments the
                                   // picture number
```

```
protected:
   int PictureNumber;      // holds current film position

};

void AutoWindCamera::TakePicture()
{
   // use scope resolution operator to call
   // the base class TakePicture() function
   Camera::TakePicture();

   PictureNumber += 1;     // OK! PictureNumber is
                           // protected in Camera class
}
```

It is worth noting at this point that we have now changed the interface specification of a base class. Thus, any other source code and derived classes of the **Camera** base class must be recompiled before being used. It is not sufficient to change only the header file containing the class declaration.

Member functions can also be declared as protected. For example, suppose the **AdvanceFilm()** method in the **Camera** class should only be called by other class methods or by instances of its derived classes. Then it should be declared **protected**, so other unrelated classes and functions cannot call it:

```
class Camera
{
public:
   virtual void TakePicture();    // snaps a picture

protected:
   void AdvanceFilm();     // increments the
                           // picture number
private:
   int PictureNumber;      // holds current film position

};
```

If we try to call **AdvanceFilm()** outside the class now, we get another compiler error:

```
Camera c;

c.TakePicture();
c.AdvanceFilm();       // ERROR! method is protected
```

Note that **AdvanceFilm()** controls the value of **PictureNumber**, so the variable can be declared **private**. Derived classes can call **AdvanceFilm()** to increment the variable instead of accessing the variable directly:

```
void AutoWindCamera::TakePicture()
{
    // use scope resolution operator to call
    // the base class TakePicture() function
    Camera::TakePicture();

    PictureNumber += 1;    // ERROR! PictureNumber is
                           // private in Camera class

    AdvanceFilm();         // OK! AdvanceFilm() is
                           // a protected method
}
```

You can get by without using the protected keyword for data by providing public or protected get and set member functions to access or change the private data. The get and set functions can then do error checking and protect the state of the object from invalid changes, while controlling access from derived classes. However, the price to pay for this encapsulation is the task of writing these functions. And these additional methods increase the complexity and size of the class, although this can be alleviated somewhat by the use of inline methods.

Protected and Private Inheritance

Up to now, derived classes have been presented using **public** inheritance:

```
class X : public Y
{
    // ...
};
```

With **public** class inheritance, derived classes can access both the public and protected members of the base class. So any new methods in class X can access any public or protected members of Y, and instances of class X can call the public methods of both X and Y.

The **protected** and **private** access specifiers can also be used for specifying base class inheritance:

```
class X : protected Y
{
    // ...
};
```

When X inherits from Y with protected inheritance, the public and protected members of Y can be accessed from within X. But these members become protected in X, so classes derived from X inherit the public members of Y as rprotected members. Thus, instances of class X can no longer access the public members of Y. Of course, instances of Y can still access the public parts of Y. But X has hidden these members from users of the X class:

```
class X : private Y
{
    // ...
};
```

With private inheritance, the public and protected members of Y continue to be accessible within X, but these members become private to X. Thus, they cannot be inherited from classes that are subsequently derived from X. Nor can these members be accessed by users of X.

In general, it is a good idea to use public inheritance most of the time. Otherwise, subsequent derived classes may not be able to access the public methods of the base classes in the class hierarchy. Of course, there may be times when it is desirable to hide a previously public interface in a derived class, but public inheritance is the rule in most programs.

Unfortunately, if you omit the access specifier in the class declaration, the default is private inheritance. Thus, it is important to include the access keyword when writing your class declarations.

Summary

We have introduced the **protected** access specifier and presented examples to illustrate how protected variables let derived classes access data in base classes. We have explained the use of get and set functions to access protected data members and discussed public, protected, and private class inheritance.

CHAPTER 15

MORE ON VIRTUAL FUNCTIONS

I deeply grieve to say that in declining to entertain my last application to myself, I presumed to address myself in terms which render it impossible for me ever to apply to myself again.
Iolanthe

The concept of virtual functions is worth a bit more discussion. You can declare methods of a base class as virtual if

1. the method is a public or protected member of the base class and

2. a future derived class may overload the base class method with a new implementation.

In this chapter, we will use a new example base class, **ChessPiece**, and a derived class **Pawn**. We'll also define an enumerated type to denote the color of the chess piece. Here is the declaration and implementation of the base class:

```
enum Color { black, white };

class ChessPiece
{

public:
    // constructor and destructor
    ChessPiece(Color c, int row, char col);
    virtual ~ChessPiece() {}

    // move piece to new position
    virtual void Move(int row, char col);

    // pure virtual function
    virtual void Draw() = 0;

protected:
    // method to return the color
    inline Color Side() const { return myColor; }

    int myRow;        // current position
    char myCol;
```

```
private:
    Color myColor;    // color of piece
};

// constructor
ChessPiece::ChessPiece(Color c, int row, char col)
{
    myColor = c;
    myRow = row;
    myCol = col;
}

// Move - moves the piece to a new location
void ChessPiece::Move(int row, char col)
{
    myRow = row;
    myCol = col;
}
```

Pawn is a derived class of **ChessPiece**:

```
class Pawn : public ChessPiece
{

public:
    // constructor and destructor
    Pawn(Color c, int row, char col);
    ~Pawn() {}

    // pawn move function
    void Move(int row, char col);

protected:
    void Draw();    // pawn draw function

private:
    int EnPassant;    // 1 if En Passant capture is
                      // legal, 0 if not

};
```

Constructors and Destructors

There are several rules and guidelines illustrated by this class hierarchy. One is that constructors are never declared virtual. You cannot override a base class constructor with a derived class constructor. Rather, your derived class constructor calls the base class constructor first. Then the derived class constructor code is executed.

For example, the **Pawn** constructor is implemented as follows:

```
Pawn::Pawn(Color c, int row, char col)
    : ChessPiece(c, row, col)
```

```
{
    EnPassant = 0;
}
```

When a **Pawn** object is constructed, the **ChessPiece** constructor is called first, followed by the **Pawn** constructor. The syntax in writing derived class constructors is to declare the derived class constructor, followed by a colon and the base class constructor, passing any required arguments to the base class constructor. In this case, the base class constructor is called with the same arguments that are passed to the **Pawn** constructor. After the base class constructor is finished, the **Pawn** constructor finishes by setting the **EnPassant** variable to zero.

The next thing to notice about **ChessPiece** is that the destructor is declared **virtual**. You can make a general rule that *all base class destructors should be declared virtual*. If not, and a destructor is implemented on an object whose type is not known at compile time, the destructors will not be called in the proper sequence.

For example, in a chess program with no virtual destructor for **ChessPiece**, the following function will not call the derived class destructor as it should:

```
void Capture(ChessPiece *c)
{
    // if the ChessPiece destructor is not virtual,
    // then passing a Pawn object to this function
    // will not call the Pawn destructor!
    delete c;    // uh, oh!
}
```

```
// declare a new Pawn object and call the
// Capture function

Pawn *p1 = new Pawn(black, 2, 'b');
Capture(p1);
```

The function destroys the chess piece object by calling the **delete** operator. Thus, the **ChessPiece** destructor is called. But we want to call the **Pawn** destructor first, followed by the **ChessPiece** destructor. The trouble is that the **Capture()** function does not know a pawn object has been passed to it until run time. Unless the **ChessPiece** destructor is declared virtual, the delete operation will not call the **Pawn** destructor.

However, if the destructor is declared virtual in the base class, then the **delete** operator in the **Capture()** function will call the **Pawn** destructor first. The base class destructor ~**ChessPiece**() is then called. Thus, the virtual destructors are called in reverse order from the constructors for derived class objects.

To summarize, if you define constructors for a derived class, all of the derived class constructors must call the base class constructor first. Base class constructors are invoked by putting the base constructor call immediately after the derived class constructor function declaration, separated by a colon. So base class constructors are called before the derived class constructor code is executed. This ensures that all inherited base class variables are initialized properly before the derived class accesses any of them.

All base class destructors should be declared virtual. When a derived class destructor is called, the code for the derived class destructor will be executed, followed by the destructors for the base classes. Thus, the calling order of destructors is the opposite of the calling order for constructors. Derived classes therefore get a chance to clean up any allocated memory, open files, etc., before the base class destructors are called.

When to Use Virtual Functions

In the **ChessPiece** class, most of the functions are declared virtual, but the functions are not declared virtual in the derived class **Pawn**. The reason is that only base class functions need the virtual declaration. Inherited methods that were virtual in the base class continue to be virtual in the derived class and in other classes which are further derived. However, even though we have not used the virtual keyword in the **Pawn** class, it is probably a good idea to continue the virtual declarations. The author of future derived classes need only look at the declaration of one class to determine which functions are virtual.

There is also no reason to declare a private function of a class virtual. No other derived classes or objects outside the class can override a private class method anyway, so there is nothing to be gained from the virtual declaration.

In general, if there is a possibility of deriving future classes from a class, then the public and protected functions of the class that might be redefined in future derived classes should be declared virtual. All functions in **ChessPiece** except for **Side()** (and the constructor) were declared virtual. **Side()** does not need the virtual declaration because derived classes do not need to change its implementation, which merely returns the color of the piece.

On the other hand, **Move()** is defined in the base class, but every different kind of **ChessPiece** has specific legal moves, so **Move()** will probably be redefined in every derived class so that legal and illegal moves can be trapped. Therefore, the **ChessPiece::Move()** function is declared virtual.

Pure Virtual Methods

The last specific point to notice about the **ChessPiece** class declaration is the statement

```
virtual void Draw() = 0;
```

This use of assignment with a virtual class method declaration signifies that the function is a *pure virtual function*. That is, the **Draw()** function for the **ChessPiece** class must be defined by whatever classes are derived from this base class. No implementation for pure virtual functions is required when writing the class, so there is no **ChessPiece::Draw()** source code (you can in fact write source code for pure virtual functions, but we will not consider that here).

If a class does contain a pure virtual function, the class cannot be instantiated directly in a program. The class is referred to as an *abstract base class*. For example, it makes no sense for a chess program to instantiate an object of type **ChessPiece**, because chess programs work with specific types of chess pieces, namely pawns, kings, rooks, etc. Thus, the following statements are illegal:

```
// ILLEGAL! ChessPiece is an abstract base class
ChessPiece p1(black, 2, 'a');
ChessPiece *piece = new ChessPiece(white, 7, 'e');
```

Note that it is still legal for a function to take a pointer to an abstract base class as an argument. But the actual pointers passed to the function will point to instances of derived classes of the abstract base class. Thus, the declaration of the **Capture()** function above is valid.

If a derived class defines a new **Draw()** method that overrides the pure virtual **Draw()** function in the base class, instances of the derived class can be declared. For instance, define **Draw()** for the **Pawn** class as

```
void Pawn::Draw()
{
    cout << "P";
}
```

and the following declarations are legal:

```
Pawn p(black, 7, 'c');
Pawn *p = new Pawn(white, 2, 'h');
```

If the **Draw()** function is not declared and defined in **Pawn**, then **Pawn** too will be an abstract base class.

Performance Issues

To be completely general in declaring virtual functions, you may simply decide to adopt the convention of declaring all public and protected methods virtual. This may arguably be a good policy, but it has some effects on the performance of your application.

The declaration of one or more functions as virtual causes the C++ compiler to set up a virtual function pointer table for the class. This causes a level of indirection for virtual function calls. An indirect function call through a function pointer may take longer (although this may be compiler and system dependent). Therefore, virtual functions can impose a performance penalty.

Consider a system where a virtual function call is 15% slower than a direct function call. For an application with 20% of its performance tied up in function calls and all function calls virtual, the overall performance penalty for virtual functions will be about 3%. On the other hand, an application with 80% of its time spent making function calls on a system where virtual functions take twice as long will show a performance penalty of 80%.

Summary

Virtual function concepts were developed further. We introduced pure virtual functions and abstract base classes and presented some guidelines on when virtual functions are required. Performance issues relative to the use of virtual functions were discussed.

CHAPTER 16

THE this KEYWORD

They give me this and they give me that,
And I've nothing whatever to grumble at!
Princess Ida

It is sometimes desirable for an object to refer to itself. What does that mean? How can a method inside of a class refer to the instance of the class itself?

In Smalltalk, an object refers to itself with the keyword **self**. The **this** keyword does the same thing in C++. **this** is only valid inside a class method and refers to the particular instance of the class that is being used. An example will serve to explain the concept of self-reference.

Back to Strings

The **String** class developed earlier will be used for our example. Here is a string class declaration and implementation:

```
class String
{

public:
    // constructor and destructor
    String(char *p);
    ~String() { delete [] s; }

    // return length, pointer to char array
    inline int Len() const { return length; }
    inline char *Str() { return s; }

private:
    char *s;
    int length;

};


String::String(char *p)
{
    // get length of input array
```

```
        length = strlen(p) + 1;

        // allocate memory and copy input data
        s = new char[length];
        strcpy(s, p);
};
```

Although we haven't mentioned it before, the constructor and all other methods in a class have an implicit argument passed to them as the first argument in the list. This implicit argument is a pointer to the instance of the class, which is defined by the keyword **this**. So internally, the compiler sees the constructor code as

```
String::String(String *this, char *p)
{
    this->length = strlen(p) + 1;
    this->s = new char[this->length];
    strcpy(this->s, p);
}
```

Each method in the class effectively receives a pointer to a particular instance of the class (or structure) as an argument. C++ generates the implicit pointer argument and code syntax automatically, so you never have to actually code **this** when referencing class methods or variables.

However, it turns out to be useful in some cases to use self-reference directly in a class implementation. Let's extend the **String** class with another function, **Concatenate()**, which will add another string to the current string, and return a reference to the modified current string.

The prototype in the class definition will be

```
String& Concatenate(String& add_me);
```

and the implementation is

```
String& String::Concatenate(String& add_me)
{
    // compute total length
    length += add_me.Len() + 1;

    // allocate memory and copy the current string
    char *tmp = new char[length];
    strcpy(tmp, s);

    // concatenate the string passed in
    strcat(tmp, add_me.Str());

    delete [] s;    // delete old string
    s = tmp;        // current string is now modified
```

```
    // return current instance of String
    return *this;
}
```

As the function needs to return a reference to the current object, the return value is just the **this** pointer, dereferenced with the * operator (used just as if referring to the value of any pointer). The **Concatenate()** function can now be used in a program as follows:

```
#include <iostream.h>

void main()
{
    // declare 4 instances of string
    String s1("Jump");
    String s2(" Start");
    String s3(" C++");
    String s4(" Course");

    s1.Concatenate(s2);    // s1="Jump Start"
    s1.Concatenate(s3);    // s1="Jump Start C++"
    s1.Concatenate(s4);    // s1="Jump Start C++ Course"

    cout << s1 << endl;
    return 0;
}
```

The main program is perfectly straightforward, but it makes no use of our return value from **Concatenate()**. An alternative way to concatenate the strings together makes use of the ***this** return value:

```
s1.Concatenate(s2).Concatenate(s3).Concatenate(s4).
```

Now the **Concatenate(s3)** method is called on the object returned by **s1.Concatenate(s2)**, which is **s1**! Similarly, **Concatenate(s4)** is called by the object returned by the concatenation of **s3**, which again is **s1**. So **this** has been used to simplify the way the user of the class calls a class method.

A more typical use of **this** is in the definition of the assignment operator (**operator=**) for a class. Defining **operator=** to return a reference to the class instance using ***this** enables chaining together assignment statements similar to the way built-in types use chained assignment:

```
long i, j, k;
i = j = k = 0;
```

Summary

We defined the keyword **this** and showed how self-reference can be used in an example string class to simplify use of a class method in an application program.

CHAPTER 17

OBJECT-ORIENTED DESIGN

I recognize you now -- you are the picture that hangs at the end of the gallery.
   In a bad light, I am.
Ruddigore

Up to now, we have been designing and writing C++ classes without any formal specification procedure. The variables and methods needed to implement simple classes are mostly obvious. String classes need a character array, a complex number class requires two doubles to represent the real and imaginary components of the number, etc. The objects in most real world applications are not quite so simple, or at least not quite so obvious as to how they should best be implemented.

There are a few steps which can help in the process of designing object-oriented implementations for applications. While a formal specification process can and often does get carried too far, keeping in mind five design principles will enable you to get started on any project.

A Stepwise Approach

We describe five steps to follow in setting up objects for your applications and discuss an example object-oriented design exercise to acquaint you with their use.

Step 1 -- Identify Objects

First, identify the entities that are part of your application domain. These are the nouns you use to describe the application. For example, an airport application deals with runways, planes, passengers, luggage, etc. These nouns become the objects in your object-oriented design.

Step 2 -- List Behaviors

Second, list the behaviors of each entity. For each object in step 1, there are verbs that describe what actions each object can take. Continuing the airport application example, verbs that are associated with planes include take-off, land, etc. Passengers pick up luggage, board, and disembark. The verbs become the member functions of your object.

Step 3 -- Classify Relationships

Third, classify the relationships between the objects. Take the objects (nouns) that you identified in step 1 and determine whether the objects have no relationship to one another, IS-A relationships, or HAS-A relationships.

An IS-A relationship is one where one object IS-A type or subtype of another object. For example, a Boeing 747 IS-A Airplane, a Pilot IS-A CrewMember, etc. IS-A relationships define the class hierarchy or multiple class hierarchies that describe general and specific type relationships among the application objects.

HAS-A relationships denote that an object is contained in or is part of another object. A Passenger HAS-A set of luggage, an Airport HAS-A runway, etc. This type of container or owner relationship denotes that these objects should be member variables of the object that contains them.

Step 4 -- Design the Classes

Fourth, design the C++ classes through standard class declarations. Start by drawing a class hierarchy based on the IS-A relationships you found in step 3. The trick here is to keep the most abstract or general classes at the top of the hierarchy. Derived classes should begin to reflect more specialized types of objects, with increasing specialization at the bottom of the class tree.

As an example, consider a class hierarchy of air vehicles. There may be some generic class, perhaps called **AirVehicle**, at the top of the class hierarchy, with subclasses consisting of various subtypes such as **Helicopter**, **Airplane**, **Ultralight**, etc. Under **Airplane**, there may be types such as **Glider**, **Prop** and **Jet**. Under **Jet** may be types such as **J707**, **J747**, etc. Depending on the problem you want to model, you may choose to organize such a class hierarchy differently. Perhaps **AirVehicle** could be broken into subtypes such as **Military** or **Civilian** or as **Passenger**, **Freight**, **Utility**, **Fighter**, **Bomber**, etc.

Once you have defined the class hierarchy, you can write a preliminary set of C++ class declarations. These declarations should reflect the inheritance structure of the class hierarchy. Each class should show member functions for the object behaviors using the verbs identified in step 2. Also, member variables for any objects contained in the class (the HAS-A relationships from step 3) should be included in the protected or private parts of the class.

Step 5 -- Iterate

Finally, examine your design and determine if the objects and their behavior represent an adequate model of the application domain. It is very important to iterate your design until it suits the requirements the application program must meet. This may mean totally restructuring your class hierarchy or viewing the problem differently with a whole new set of objects.

An Example Problem

It is important to remember that good design, and especially good object-oriented design, is more art than science. It takes practice and good anticipatory skills to design classes that solve the current problem, yet remain general enough to permit code reuse, extensibility, and modification for future similar and unrelated projects.

With that caveat in mind, we will now examine a particular problem to illustrate the steps in an object-oriented design. After reading through the following discussion, we encourage you to develop your own solution to the problem. It will probably differ from the one presented here, but neither one is likely to be "best" in every sense.

The problem we will examine is the following: Design a model for different types of economic business units, showing the relationships between the units and some simple properties (e.g., name, assets, expenses, sales). Include methods for computing the profit for each type of business unit.

A Solution

In step 1, we must identify the nouns in the problem. The most important ones are types of business units. We will use conglomerate, company, division, and alliance. Next, we identify other nouns: the name of the business, the current assets, the amount of expenses, gross sales, number of employees, etc.

Here is the list of nouns, or objects, that we will consider for this example:

- conglomerate
- name of business
- number of employees
- company
- assets
- owner

- division
- expenses
- alliance
- sales

For step 2, we associate actions with the objects. We only consider actions taken by the business units for this example. These actions include the following, which will become member functions of the objects:
- make sales
- pay bills
- compute profit
- hire and fire employees

Conglomerates also buy and sell companies, and companies create and sell off divisions, so these actions will be associated with their objects.

For step 3, we determine the relationships among the objects in step 1. Let's look at HAS-A relationships first. It is obvious that all four of our business types (conglomerate, company, division, and alliance) contain or have properties such as name, assets, expenses, etc. So we can write
- (conglomerate, company, division, alliance) HAS-A (name, assets, expenses, sales, employees, owner)

Also note the relationships between the business types. A conglomerate contains a set of companies, a company contains divisions, and an alliance is a company with two owners (for the purposes of this example):
- conglomerate HAS-A company(s)
- company HAS-A division(s)
- alliance HAS-A second owner

Now consider the IS-A, or subtype, relationships. An alliance is a type of company with more than one owner, so we can write
- alliance IS-A company

In some solutions to this problem, a division might be considered a type of company, but we have set up a company to contain divisions, so that is a HAS-A rather than an IS-A relationship.

Moving on to step 4, we can draw a class hierarchy as in Figure 1. We can also start to set up the C++ classes at this point. However, we can simplify all of the class definitions by examining Figure 1 closely.

Note that the top level of our class structure contains three classes: conglomerate, company, and division, which do not appear related. But in step 3, we found a HAS-A relationship where all three objects and the subobject alliance all share a common set of attributes (name, assets, expenses, etc.). Thus, we can define a generic class that holds these attributes and let conglomerate, company, and division be derived from it.

This generic class will be called BusinessUnit and will be defined as an abstract base class. Conglomerate, Company, and Division will each be derived from the BusinessUnit class. The new IS-A relationship is written

- (conglomerate, company, division) IS-A business unit

Figure 1. Sample class hierarchy for the business model

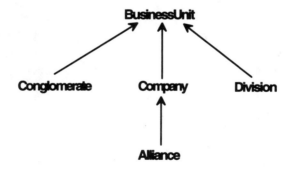

Figure 2. Modified business unit class hierarchy

The modified class hierarchy is shown in Figure 2. Now we can continue by writing the class definitions. Start at the top of the hierarchy with the **BusinessUnit** class:

```
// an abstract base class
```

```
class BusinessUnit
{

public:
    // constructor and destructor
    BusinessUnit(char *name, char *owner);
    virtual ~BusinessUnit();

    // actions
    virtual void Receive(float money);
    virtual void Pay(float money);
    virtual void Hire(int num);
    virtual void Fire(int num);

    // compute profitability (note this is a
    // pure virtual function)
    virtual float Profit() = 0;

protected:
    char *myName;
    char *myOwner;
    float myAssets;
    float myExpenses;
    float mySales;
    int NumEmployees;

};
```

We have declared the member variables with protected access, so the derived classes can access them directly, but they remain private outside of our class hierarchy. Four actions, or member functions, have been defined from the verbs we listed in step 2. The original problem statement asked for a function to compute profit. Thus, a pure virtual function, **Profit()**, was declared so that **BusinessUnit** will be an abstract base class. We must define the profit computation for each derived class by overriding the base class **Profit()** function.

Here is the class declaration for **Conglomerate**, which is derived from **BusinessUnit**:

```
class Conglomerate : public BusinessUnit
{

public:
    // constructor and destructor
    Conglomerate(char *name, char *owner);
    virtual ~Conglomerate();

    // actions
    void BuyCompany(Company& c);
    void SellCompany(Company& c);

    // override the base class pure
    // virtual function
    float Profit();
```

```
private:
    int NumCompanies;      // number of companies
    Company *list;         // array of companies

};
```

Private variables hold the array of companies that make up the conglomerate, with the contents of the array controlled by the actions **BuyCompany()** and **SellCompany()**. You may decide to compute the profitability of a conglomerate by summing the profits of all companies in the array, so the **Profit()** function could be defined as

```
float Conglomerate::Profit()
{
    float total = 0.0;
    for (int i = 0; i < NumCompanies; i++)
        total += list[i].Profit();

    return total;
}
```

The class declaration for **Company** could be written as

```
class Company : public BusinessUnit
{

public:
    // constructor and destructor
    Company(char *name, char *owner);
    virtual ~Company();

    // actions
    void CreateDivision(Division& d);
    void SellOffDivision(Division& d);

    // override the base class pure
    // virtual function
    float Profit();
protected:
    int NumDivisions;      // number of divisions
    Division *list;        // array of divisions

};
```

We declare the variables holding the number and array of divisions as protected because **Alliance** will be derived from **Company**. We also need to declare member functions to create and sell off divisions and a member function to compute the profit of the company. A company's profit could simply be the sum of profits from each division:

```
float Company::Profit()
```

```
{
    float total = 0.0;
    for (int i = 0; i < NumDivisions; i++)
        total += list[i].Profit();

    return total;
}
```

At this point, the code is practically writing itself. The next class is **Division**, which only needs an action that computes the profit of a division. This can simply be the expenses subtracted from the gross sales. The **Division** class and profit function is written as

```
class Division : public BusinessUnit
{

public:
    // constructor and destructor
    Division(char *name, char *owner);
    virtual ~Division();

    // override base class pure
    // virtual function
    float Profit();

};


float Division::Profit()
{
    return(mySales - myExpenses);
}
```

The last class in the hierarchy is **Alliance**, which is even simpler. **Alliance** can inherit the **Profit()** function from **Company**, so it doesn't need to define its own. It does require another variable, however, to represent the second owner. The constructor also takes an extra argument representing the second owner:

```
class Alliance : public Company
{

public:
    // constructor and destructor
    Alliance(char *name, char *owner1, char *owner2);
    virtual ~Alliance();

private:
    char *mySecondOwner;    // second owner

};
```

If you find the design satisfactory for the application, you should next fill in the code for the member functions we did not define and use the classes in a main program. Do not be afraid to go back and change your design if it does not address all requirements of the application. It is rare to get a design completely right the first time.

Exercises

1. Develop a class hierarchy which models the types of PC workstations available today. Include variables for the processor type, model number, clock speed, type of bus (e.g., microchannel or AT-bus), operating system, display type, and price.

2. Write a C++ class to read a binary data file written by some vendor's application. The data are in the following format:

```
// data format is a header, followed by an array of
// (x,y) data points
struct Hdr {
    int version      // version of program = 100
    int npts;        // number of (x,y) points
}
x0              // float x0, y0, ...
y0
x1
y1
...
```

Now, the vendor provides a new version of the application which uses a new header but has the same data format. Derive a class from the one you wrote above and use it to write a conversion program to convert old files to the new format:

```
struct Hdr2 {
    int version;            // version of program = 200
    int npts;               // number of (x,y) points
    char description[25]    // a text field
};
```

Summary

In this chapter, we presented a set of five steps to follow for object-oriented design:

1. Identify the nouns (objects) in the application domain.

2. List the behavior or services of each object (verbs) which become the class member functions.

3. Classify the relationships between objects as IS-A or HAS-A.

4. Design C++ classes by drawing a class hierarchy and writing the class definitions based on the results of steps 1, 2, and 3.

5. Iterate the design until it works.

We illustrated how to use these steps on a sample business unit model problem.

CHAPTER 18

PROGRAMMING STYLE IN C++

In a contemplative fashion, And a tranquil frame of mind, Free from every kind of passion, Some solution let us find.
The Gondoliers

Thus far, we have seen a number of examples of programming methods and approaches in C++. In this chapter, we will try to bring these elements together using a somewhat more extensive programming example.

We have seen that C++ programs are composed primarily of classes or *objects* and that standard function calls are frequently replaced by member functions. In fact, this leads to a number of changes in programming style which can make programs both more readable and easier to write:

1. Programs are made up primarily of classes.

2. Objects themselves contain persistent data values.

3. These data values are accessed primarily with **Get** and **Set** functions.

4. Member functions often have no arguments since they operate on data contained in the object.

5. The **switch** statement is used much less often: new classes are derived from base classes instead, with new virtual functions.

The Printer Base Class

Let us begin designing a program which will allow us to print in normal or compressed type, with and without underlining on any of a number of types of printers. Some of the most common categories of printers include IBM-compatible dot matrix (which IBM calls PPDS), HP Laserjet compatible (which Hewlett-Packard calls PCL), and PostScript printers. There are, in addition, a number of variations on all three types.

Both PPDS and PCL printers utilize *escape codes to* control printing functions. These codes are sequences of characters preceded by the Escape character (decimal 27 or octal 33). Some of the common escape sequences are shown in Table 1. In the **printf** format syntax, you can represent the numerical value of individual bytes in octal by preceding the 3-digit octal number with a backslash.

Printer Escape Codes		
	IBM Dot Matrix (PPDS)	HP Laserjet (PCL)
Set 10 cpi	'\022"	*Esc*(s0T
Set 17 cpi	'\017"	*Esc*(s16H
Start Underline	*Esc* - "\1"	*Esc*&dD
End Underline	*Esc* -"\0"	*Esc*&d@

Because PostScript printers are more complex, we will leave a description of PostScript printing for the following chapter and not develop code for their use here.

Now in a typical C program, we would handle these different types of printers using a **switch** statement:

```
void startunderline(int ptype, FILE *f)
{
  switch (ptype)
    {
    case DOTMATRIX:
        fputs("\033-\1", f);
    case HPLASER:
        fputs("\033&dD, f);
    }
}
```

Public Parts of the Printer Class

However, in C++, we will handle them by creating a base **Printer** class and then deriving classes from it for each printer type. We start by defining the public members of the base class. It should contain the usual constructor and destructor:

```
Printer(const clString&)     //constructor
virtual ~Printer();          //destructor
```

The string passed to the constructor will be the name of the device or file where the data are to be printed. This string is a member of the class **clString** which we defined in Chapter 8.

We will also need to have a function to query the error state of the printer:

```
PrtLibErr Error();                    //return error state
```

It will return one of the errors of the enumerated type **PrtLibErr**:

```
enum PrtLibErr {PRT_NONE, PRT_ILLEGALDEVICE,
                PRT_DEVICENOTOPEN, PRT_DEVICENOTREADY};
```

Then, we will need two print functions: one which prints text and one which prints text and a carriage return as well as a page eject function:

```
virtual void PrintLine(const clString& l);// with cr-lf
virtual void PrintText(const clString& ); //no cr-lf
virtual void Page_Eject(); //has defaults but can change
```

We declare these last two functions as **virtual** so that they can be redefined in derived classes. However, since the underline and character size setting functions are completely printer dependent, we make these *pure virtual functions*, which must be defined in derived classes:

```
//pure virtual functions
virtual void Start_Underline() = 0;
virtual void End_Underline() = 0;
virtual void Set17Cpi() = 0;
virtual void Set10Cpi() = 0;
```

The Private Part of the Printer Class

Possibly, the only variables we need in the private part of the printer class are ones that keep track of the printer file stream pointer, error state, and perhaps, a line counter:

```
private:
  int linecount;      //number of lines printed on page
  PrtLibErr err;      //error state
  FILE *lp;           //file stream pointer
```

Depending on how elaborate you are making your printer classes, you might also include variables to contain the current character width and line width.

The Base Printer Class Member Functions

It is not too difficult to write the basic functions we have outlined for the printer class. The constructor must open the specified printer device as a file. We will use the standard C file functions here. We discuss the iostream file member functions in the following chapter.

The printer constructor tries to open the file using the device name specified: for example "lpt1". It sets the error code if the file cannot be opened:

```
//----------constructor----------------
Printer::Printer(const clString& lpfile)
{
lp = fopen(lpfile.GetStr(), "w");        //open device
if (lp == 0)
   err = PRT_ILLEGALDEVICE; //error if NULL
else
   err=PRT_NONE;
}
```

Note that we pass in the device name as an instance of type **clString** and that we use the **GetStr()** member function to obtain the **char** pointer that the C **fopen** function requires. Note also that we pass in this variable by reference using the **&** symbol and that we use the **const** modifier to indicate that the **clString** object cannot be modified.

As you see, both the file stream pointer **lp** and the error variable **err** are inside the class. You set the file handle when you invoke the constructor and the error variable is set by each operation.

The analogous destructor closes the file and ejects the final page:

```
//--------destructor-----------------
Printer::~Printer()
{
if (lp != 0)
   {
   Page_Eject();       //eject last page
   fclose(lp);         //close the output file
   }
}
```

The **PrintText** member function simply calls the **fputs** function,

```
void Printer::PrintText(const clString& text)
{
if(lp != 0)
   {
   int perr=fputs(text.GetStr(), lp);
   if (perr != 0)
      err = PRT_DEVICENOTREADY
    else
    err = PRT_NONE
   }
else
   err = PRT_DEVICENOTOPEN;
}
```

and sets the error variable if the device is not open or if the output fails.

The **PrintLine** member function utilizes the overloaded "+" operator in the **clString** class to concatentate the text string with a newline character:

```
void Printer::PrintLine(const clString& line)
{
PrintText(line + clString("\n"));  //append newline
}
```

Finally, the **Page_Eject** function simply sends the form feed character to the printer.:

```
void Printer::Page_Eject()
{
PrintText(clString("\f"));  //form feed character
}
```

The form feed character will cause a page eject on all dot matrix and PCL printers but will not work for PostScript printers. Consequently, we have declared this member function as **virtual** so we can replace it in the derived class for PostScript printers.

Dot Matrix Printers

Most dot matrix printers respond to the IBM-compatible (PPDS) codes, and we will use them as the example here. We first create a *derived class* called **DotMatrix**:

```
class DotMatrix:public Printer
{
public:
   DotMatrix(const clString&);      // constructor
   ~DotMatrix();                    // destructor
    void Start_Underline();         // derived versions
    void End_Underline();
    void Set17Cpi();
    void Set10Cpi();
};
```

Now we have derived the class **DotMatrix** from the class **Printer**. We specify that **DotMatrix** has **public** inheritance from **Printer**, which means that all public members in the base class remain public in the derived class.

We need only declare the member functions that we will derive from those in the base class and any new private variables we might need for this class of printer. Since we made the underline and character size functions pure virtual, we *must* declare them and write actual functions for them if we plan to create instances of the derived class. The actual underline functions for this class are

```
//-----------DotMatrix::Start_Underline----------------
void DotMatrix::Start_Underline()
{
PrintText("\033-\1");
}
//-----------DotMatrix::End_Underline-----------------
```

```
void DotMatrix::End_Underline()
{
PrintText("\033-\0");
}
```

and the character size functions are

```
//-----------DotMatrix::Set10Cpi---------------------------
void DotMatrix::Set10Cpi()
{
PrintText("\022");
}
//----------DotMatrix::Set17Cpi---------------------------
void DotMatrix::Set17Cpi()
{
PrintText("\017");
}
```

The DotMatrix Class Constructor

The constructor for this derived class is as follows:

```
//-----------DotMatrix::Constructor-----------------
DotMatrix::DotMatrix(const clString& lp):Printer(lp)
{
Set10Cpi();
}
```

First, it passes the constant string **lp** to the constructor for the **Printer** class, and then it initializes the printer by setting it to 10 cpi. In a more elaborate library, you might also initialize the font, print quality, margin settings, line count, and paper length.

The Main Printing Program

Now that we have declared a complete class, we can write a simple program to print out some text, both underlined and non underlined. This program is quite simple:

```
void main ()
{
DotMatrix dm("lpt1");
dm.PrintText("This is the plain text. ");
dm.Start_Underline();
dm.PrintText("This is underlined. ");
dm.End_Underline();
dm.PrintLine("This is not");
}
```

It opens device **lpt1** and prints a normal line of text, an underlined phrase, and the remainder of the line again without underscoring:

```
This is the plain text. This is underlined. This is not.
```

An HP LaserJet Printer Class

We can create a new derived printer class in much the same way. The class declaration is virtually identical:

```
class HPLaser : public Printer
{
public:
    HPLaser(const clString&);
    ~HPLaser();
    void Start_Underline();
    void End_Underline();
    void Set17Cpi();
    void Set10Cpi();
};
```

and the underlining and character width functions are quite similar:

```
//-------------HPLaser::Set10Cpi---------------------------
void HPLaser::Set10Cpi()
{
PrintText("\033(s0T");
}
//-------------HPLaser::Set17Cpi---------------------------
void HPLaser::Set17Cpi()
{
PrintText("\033(s16H");
}
//-------------HPLaser::Start_Underline-------------------
void HPLaser::Start_Underline()
{
PrintText("\033&dD");
}
//------------HPLaser::Start_Underline-----,-------------
void HPLaser::End_Underline()
{
PrintText("\033&d@");
}
```

The constructor is also nearly the same, except that we specifically reset the printer with the *Esc*E code, after the base **Printer** constructor has opened the output device:

```
//-------------constructor--------------------------
HPLaser::HPLaser(const clString& device):Printer(device)
{
PrinText("\033E");
Set10Cpi();
}
```

DAY 3

REVIEW

In the previous day's work, we discussed copy constructors and assignment operators and learned how to use the **const** declaration to protect structures which are passed by reference. Then we discussed inheritance, private and protected class members, and virtual functions. We introduced the concept of the **this** pointer and went through a detailed design exercise, so that we could understand relationships between derived classes.

In the Day 3 work, we will discuss how you can utilize files in C++ and introduce the concept of **friend** classes and functions. Then, we will introduce **static** members and illustrate the concept of templates with a simple example. Finally we will take up the idea of multiple inheritance and go over some guidelines for general C++ programming.

CHAPTER 19

FILES AND STREAMS

Your silent matches, your dark lantern seize.
Take your file and skeletonic keys.
The Pirates of Penzance

When learning a new language, it is difficult to say you really know how to program in it unless you can read and write files. Input/output (I/O) is usually left to be discussed in an appendix in most books, because it is not a formal part of the C or C++ language specification. Even though streams are merely a part of the C++ run time library, we consider them an important subject, so a couple of chapters in this book are devoted to streams.

You can use C++ file stream methods in place of the regular C file I/O functions. Thus, we will discard **fopen()**, **fclose()**, **fscanf()**, **fgets()**, **fprintf()**, **fputs()**, **fread()**, **fwrite()** and **fseek()**. In their place, we will use the classes and methods defined in *iostream.h* and *fstream.h*.

Streams are linear, ordered sequences of bytes. Data can be read from and written to streams, and streams can refer to stdin, stdout, in-memory arrays, files, or cross-platform data flows. Figure 1 shows a simplified stream class hierarchy. We have eliminated **strstream** and **stdiostream** classes from this discussion, so they don't appear in our class hierarchy. Refer to your compiler's class library guide for a more complete stream class description. Another good book on iostreams is listed in the bibliography. This chapter concentrates on the more common file stream classes and methods.

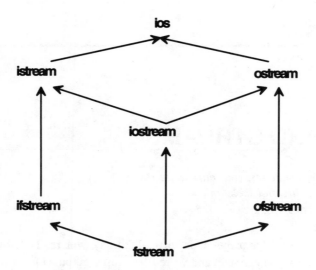

Figure 1. A simplified stream class hierarchy

The base class for all other stream classes is **ios**. This class maintains formatting and error state information for the actual stream buffers. Input (**istream**) and output (**ostream**) streams are derived from **ios**, along with an **iostream** class which inherits from both **istream** and **ostream**. This is the first case in this book where a derived class inherits from more than one base class. This is called *multiple inheritance* and is covered in more detail in a later chapter.

In addition, note the file stream classes **ifstream**, **ofstream**, and **fstream** for file I/O. We will consider these classes for file handling in this chapter.

Opening and Closing File Streams

The **ios** class defines several mode flags used in opening files. These are defined in Table 1. Some additional methods in this class query the state of a stream, allowing tests for end of file, open errors, etc. These state functions are listed in Table 2.

ios::app	seek to end of file for appending
ios::ate	seek to end of file
ios::in	open for input
ios::out	open for output
ios::trunc	existing file contents will be destroyed

ios::nocreate	open fails if file does not exist
ios::noreplace	open for writing fails if file does not exist
ios::binary	open in binary mode (text mode is the default)

Table 1. List of **ios** file open mode flags

bad()	returns true if an unrecoverable error occurs
fail() or !	returns true if unrecoverable error or file not found
good()	returns true if no error
eof()	returns true if end of file
clear()	clears all error flags

Table 2. A partial list of **ios** query state methods

In the following sections, we will present examples of how these flags and member functions are used.

Reading Text Files

An **ifstream** can be opened on a text file for reading, using any of several different constructor forms:

```
// open a file for reading
ifstream textfile("read.me", ios::in);

// default mode is ios::in
ifstream textfile("read.me");
```

You can also call the default constructor, followed by calls to the **open()** and **close()** member functions.

```
// call the default constructor
ifstream textfile;

textfile.open("read.me", ios::in);
// ...
textfile.close();
```

Of course, you can also use the extraction (>>) operator with input file streams. Another useful member function is **get()**, which will read in a single character from the stream. Using these functions, we can write a complete program which reads the contents of a text file and displays it on the screen:

```
// program to display a text file
#include <fstream.h>

int display_text(char *name)
{
    // open the text file
    ifstream in(name);
    if (!in)    // equivalent to in.fail()
        return 1;

    // read in file character by character
    // and display it
    char c;
    while ( in.get(c) )
        cout << c;

    return 0;
}
int main(int argc, char *argv[])
{
    if ( display_text(argv[1]) )
        cout << "Error accessing file"
            << endl;

    return 0;
}
```

Note that the ! operator is overloaded for streams and is equivalent to calling the **fail()** member function. This allows you to do error checking after declaring the variable, which opens the file. Thus, after **in** is declared, we can use either

```
if (!in)
    return 1;
```

or

```
if ( in.fail() )
    return 1;
```

to make sure the stream is opened with no errors.

In our example program, when the **ifstream** variable goes out of scope [after the **display_text()** function returns], the destructor is automatically called. This destructor call on the variable **in** closes the file. If we had instead used the default constructor and the **open()** member function to open the file, the **close()** method must be called explicitly:

```
int display_text(char *name)
{
    // default constructor
    ifstream in;

    // open the text file
    in.open(name);
    if (!in)    // equivalent to in.fail()
        return 1;

    // read in file character by character
    // and display it
    char c;
    while ( in.get(c) )
        cout << c;

    in.close();
    return 0;
}
```

Writing Text Files

The **ofstream** class uses the same syntax for the constructor as **ifstream,** except that the default open mode is **ios::out.** As an example of writing a text file, the following program generates a PostScript file. PostScript is a page description language from Adobe. PostScript printers interpret the commands in a PostScript text file and generate printer graphics commands which render the page contents onto a physical page.

Our application generates the PostScript file below:

```
%!PS-Adobe-1.0
%%BoundingBox: 0 0 612 792
newpath
300 400 moveto
0 72 rlineto
72 0 rlineto
0 -72 rlineto
closepath
4 setlinewidth
stroke showpage
```

When you copy these lines to a PostScript printer, the printer generates a page such as that shown in Figure 2.

Figure 2. Sample PostScript output

The complete program for drawing a PostScript box is given below:

```
// program to write a PostScript file
#include <fstream.h>

int write_text(char *name, int x, int y)
{
    // create the text file
    ofstream ps(name);
    if (!ps)     // check for errors
        return 1;

    // write the PostScript header
    ps << "%!PS-Adobe-1.0"                << endl
       << "%%BoundingBox: 0 0 612 792" << endl
       << "newpath"                        << endl;

    // draw a 1 inch square with the lower
    // left corner at x, y
    ps << x << " " << y << " moveto" << endl
       << "0 72 rlineto"                << endl
       << "72 0 rlineto"                << endl
       << "0 -72 rlineto"               << endl
       << "closepath"                   << endl;

    // set line width to 4 and draw the page
    ps << "4 setlinewidth"  << endl
       << "stroke showpage" << endl;

    return 0;
}


int main(int argc, char *argv[])
```

```
{
    if ( write_text(argv[1], 300, 400) )
        cout << "Error creating file" << endl;

    return 0;
}
```

This code is simpler looking and therefore easier to read than the corresponding C code, which would probably use **fprintf()** statements. For example, writing a string such as `"%%BoundingBox"` with **fprintf()** would actually require an output format string of `"%%%%BoundingBox"`, because '%' is a special format character in **fprintf()** format strings.

Reading Binary Files

Use the **ios::binary** mode to open a stream for binary input or output. To read binary data, you use the **read()** member function. The first argument to **read()** is a pointer to a buffer, and the second argument is the number of bytes to read into the buffer. The following example program reads data from a binary file into two arrays, where the data in the file represent (x,y) data pairs. Once the data have been read into the arrays, the main program prints out the (x,y) data values:

```
// program to read a binary file
#include <fstream.h>
int read_data(char *name, long npts,
              float *x, float *y)
{
    // open a binary file
    ifstream in(name, ios::binary);
    if (!in)    // check for errors
        return 1;

    // read data from the file
    for (long i = 0L; i < npts; i++)
    {
        in.read( (char *)&x[i], sizeof(float) );
        in.read( (char *)&y[i], sizeof(float) );
    }

    return 0;
}

int main(int argc, char *argv[])
{
    const long npts = 10;
    float x[npts], y[npts];

    // call function to read the data
    if ( read_data(argv[1], npts, x, y) )
        cout << "Error accessing file" << endl;
    else {
```

```
            // write out the contents of the array
            for (long i = 0L; i < npts; i++)
                cout << "x[" << i << "] = " << x[i] << endl
                     << "y[" << i << "] = " << y[i] << endl;
        }

    return 0;
}
```

Note that the **read()** member function needs a character array pointer as the first argument, so **&x[i]** and **&y[i]** are cast to character pointers. As the **read()** function reads bytes, you must specify the number of bytes to read with the second argument using the standard C **sizeof()** function.

Writing Binary Files

To write binary data to a file, you can use the **write()** function, which is the analog of the **read()** member function. The following program writes binary (x,y) data to an output file:

```
// program to write a binary file
#include <fstream.h>

int writedata(char *name, long npts,
              float *x, float *y)
{
    // open a binary file
    ofstream out(name, ios::out | ios::binary);
    if (!out)    // check for errors
        return 1;

    // write data to the file
    for (long i = 0L; i < npts; i++)
    {
        out.write( (char *)&x[i], sizeof(float) );
        out.write( (char *)&y[i], sizeof(float) );
    }

    return 0;
}

int main(int argc, char *argv[])
{
    const long npts = 10;
    float x[npts], y[npts];

    // initialize the x and y data arrays
    for (long i = 0L; i < npts; i++)
    {
        x[i] = (float)i;
        y[i] = (float)(i + 1L);
    }

    // call function to write the data
```

```
    if ( writedata(argv[1], npts, x, y) )
        cout << "Error accessing file" << endl;

    return 0;
}
```

Seeking and Modifying Binary Files

It is sometimes necessary to seek to a position inside an existing file and read or write data values. File streams contain an instance of a **filebuf** class internally. This internal class represents the actual stream buffer managed by the stream class. The stream buffer provides efficient, buffered input and output of the stream data.

The **filebuf** class contains a **seekoff()** member function which can be used to set the file stream pointer to any offset relative to the beginning, current position, or end of the file. The following example program illustrates how to use **seekoff()** to modify an existing binary file:

```
// program to modify a binary file
#include <fstream.h>

int chg_data(char *name, long index,
                float x, float y)
{
    // open a binary file
    fstream fdata(name, ios::in | ios::out |
                    ios::binary | ios::nocreate);
    if (!fdata)     // check for errors
        return 1;

    // compute file offset for the
    // x[index], y[index] data pair
    long offset = 2L * index * sizeof(float)

    // seek to the computed offset and write
    // the new (x,y) data values
    filebuf *buffer = fdata.rdbuf();
    buffer->seekoff(offset, ios::beg, ios::out);

    fdata.write( (char *)&x, sizeof(float) );
    fdata.write( (char *)&y, sizeof(float) );

    return 0;
}

int main(int argc, char *argv[])
{
    if ( chg_data(argv[1], 3, 50.0, 75.1) )
        cout << "Error accessing file" << endl;

    return 0;
}
```

The example shows how to use **fstream** with several **ios** mode flags ORed together. First, you compute the offset which points to the **x[index]** data value you wish to modify. Then you declare a **filebuf** pointer, initialized with a call to the **fstream** member function **rdbuf()**. Once you obtain the **filebuf** class pointer, call the **seekoff()** member function to position the stream pointer **offset** bytes from the beginning of the file. This is denoted by the second argument to **seekoff()**, **ios::beg**.

Once the file stream pointer is set to the correct position, the **write()** member function is called to overwrite the (x,y) data in the file with new values.

If we want to seek to the end of an open file, we can use the following function call, using **ios::end** to specify the end of the file:

```
// seek to end of file
buffer->seekoff(0, ios::end, ios::out);
```

Summary

This chapter dealt with how C++ streams are used to read and write files. We illustrated binary and text file I/O with complete example programs. You can use these for future reference in writing your own C++ programs.

CHAPTER 20

USING friend RELATIONSHIPS

You are very dear to me George. We were boys together, at least I was. If I were to survive you, my existence would be hopelessly embittered. **Iolanthe**

This chapter introduces the C++ keyword **friend**. Friends are a mechanism that can be used to override the encapsulation of data within an object. Friends of an object can "see" inside the object and access private and protected member functions and variables. After we introduce the syntax and show some examples, we will discuss why friends are often not such a good idea.

A C++ class can declare a friend of that class to be any of

1. a nonmember function,

2. a member function of another class, and

3. another class.

If class *A* declares another class to be a friend, the **friend** class can access the private and protected members of *A*. You declare a **friend** function or class by including the keyword **friend** inside the class definition.

In the following example, we declare a class *X* with a private variable that is initialized by the constructor. The class also declares that a nonmember function, **print_value()**, is a friend of the class:

```
class X
{

friend void print_value(X& x);

public:
        inline X(int i) { value = i; }

private:
        int value;

};
```

The **print_value()** function takes a reference to an instance of class **X** as an argument and prints out the value of **x**'s private variable:

```
void print_value(X& x)
{
     cout << "Private member of x = "
          << x.value    // private member of class X
          << endl;
}
```

Note that this will not compile unless the class includes the **friend** declaration, because **value** is private to **X** and should only be accessible to member functions of the class. As the nonmember function **print_value()** is a friend of class **X**, it has access to and can print out this private variable.

Another example illustrates how an entire class can be a friend of another class. Here is a simple declaration for a complex number class and an imaginary number class. The classes have no relationship to one another, except that **Imaginary** is declared as a friend to **Complex**:

```
class Imaginary;    // this is a forward declaration

class Complex
{
friend class Imaginary;    // the whole class is a friend
public:
     inline Complex(double r, double i)
     {
         real = r;
         imag = i;
     }
private:
     double real;
     double imag;
};


class Imaginary
{
public:
     inline Imaginary(Complex& c)
     {
         imag = c.imag;
     }
private:
```

```
    double imag;

};
```

The **Imaginary** class takes a reference to a **Complex** number class instance as a constructor argument. In the code for the **Imaginary** constructor, the private variable **imag** of **Complex** (**c.imag**) is used to initialize the private variable of the **Imaginary** class. Again, this would not compile unless **Imaginary** is declared as a friend of **Complex**. And the friend declaration must be made in the definition of the **Complex** class itself.

One other interesting point of the preceding example is that we have made a forward declaration of the **Imaginary** class. This is exactly analogous to forward references in Pascal and simply indicates to the compiler that **Imaginary** should be treated as a class, even though the compiler has not seen a declaration of the class.

Note that just because **Imaginary** is a friend of **Complex**, the reverse is not true. The **Complex** class cannot access the internals of **Imaginary** unless the **Imaginary** class also includes a friend declaration.

The Trouble with friends

Friends seem to be an easy way to expose the internals of a class and yet still maintain some control over which classes and functions are granted access. They therefore tend to be overused, particularly by beginning C++ programmers. The problem is that friends are sometimes too personal, sticking their values in where they don't belong or using methods that are inappropriate.

Friend functions or classes have unlimited access to class internals. Thus, if you make modifications to the underlying implementations or structure of class methods and variables, they may break friend class or function code that relied on the old implementation or structure. You therefore lose some of the object-oriented nature of the class structure.

Summary

This chapter discussed the concept of friend functions and friend classes. We presented an example use for forward declarations, and we showed examples and a warning against overuse of friends in C++ programs.

CHAPTER 21

STATIC MEMBERS

Perhaps you suppose this throng
Can't keep it up all day long.
If that's your idea, you're wrong, oh!
The Mikado

In C++, the **static** keyword has its usual meaning in defining the scope of variables. In addition, **static** takes on a new definition when applied to the member functions or data in a class declaration. In this chapter we explain the syntax and meaning of static members and include some examples.

In all of the class examples described so far, we have used regular, nonstatic declarations for all member functions and variables. Each instance of a class then contains its own copy of all the variables inside the class. If a class contains an integer, for example, and you declare 10 instances of the class, the compiler reserves 10 separate integer locations.

Suppose we want to create a class where all of the instances of the class refer to the same variable. The variable could be declared outside of the class definition and made static, just as in many C programs. But that exposes the variable to access and modification from any other class or function that resides in the same module as the static variable declaration.

Static Variables

C++ provides an alternate way to create a variable that all instances of a class can refer to, but still allows you to hide the variable inside the class definition. You do this using the **static** keyword on the member declaration inside the class.

For example, consider the following class, which holds an Intel x86 style near address. An Intel x86 address is composed of two parts, a two-byte segment and a two-byte offset. In near addressing, the segment remains constant and the offset ranges from 0 to 65535.

```
class NearAddress
{
public:
    // constructor
    NearAddress(unsigned int o) { offset = o; }

    // returns linear address value
    inline long Address()
    {
        return(segment*0x10L + offset);
    }

    // static variable representing segment
    // of near address
    static unsigned int segment;
private:
    unsigned int offset;    // offset of near address

};
```

Every instance of **NearAddress** contains its own individual copy of **offset**, but all instances refer to the same copy of the unsigned integer **segment**. So all instances will have the same segment address. If you change **segment**, all instances of **NearAddress** will automatically use the new value in computing the address.

Access to the segment variable inside the class is the same as that for nonstatic members. So the **Address()** function computes the linear address corresponding to a segment and offset by referring to the static variable and the instance variable normally. In the declaration above, **Address()** multiplies **segment** by 0x10 and adds the **offset** for the current instance of the class.

Notice that you do not initialize the static variable in the class definition. Rather, you should initialize it in the module that contains the class code for the other member functions. Since the class declaration and inline function definitions typically go in a header file, you usually put the source code for the other methods of the class in a separate code module. In this code module, the static class variables are initialized using the scope resolution operator. For the above example, **segment** would be initialized in the *NearAddress.C* (or *.cpp* or *.cxx*) file as follows:

```
unsigned int NearAddress::segment = 0x1000;
```

As **segment** is declared public, it can be accessed from functions outside of the class. Remember that only one copy of the static variable exists, so it cannot be referred to as a standard instance of a class variable. Instead, you must use the scope resolution operator. For example:

```
NearAddress a1(0x4000);

cout << "Segment = "
     << a1.segment    // ILLEGAL! segment is static
     << endl;
cout << "Static segment = "
     << NearAddress::segment     // OK!
     << endl;
```

Static Functions

Member functions that only operate on static variables can also be declared static. Let's modify the **NearAddress** class by changing the static variable to private and adding a function to return the value of **segment**:

```
class NearAddress
{
public:
    // constructor
    NearAddress(unsigned int o) { offset = o; }

    // returns linear address value
    inline long Address()
    {
        return(segment*0x10L + offset);
    }

    // static member function
    static unsigned int Seg();

private:
    // static variable representing segment
    // of near address
    static unsigned int segment;

    unsigned int offset;    // offset near address

};
```

The implementation of **Seg()** can be defined inline or in a code module as

```
unsigned int NearAddress::Seg()
{
    return segment;
}
```

Now a sample program can print out the segment by calling the static method using the scope resolution operator:

```
NearAddress a1(0x4000);
cout << "Segment = "
```

```
          << al.Seg()        // ILLEGAL!  static member function
          << endl;
cout << "Static segment = "
          << NearAddress::Seg()      // OK!
          << endl;
```

One important thing to remember about static functions is that they do not contain an implicit **this** pointer. Therefore, static member functions can only access static variables. They cannot access other nonstatic class members. In the **Seg()** function above, you could not use **offset** inside the function, because that variable is not static.

Reference Counting

Any class can use static variables and functions to keep track of how many instances of the class were actually used in a program. This might be done for record keeping, monitoring, or performance profiling. The following example class, **Widget**, illustrates how to add a reference count capability to any class. The definition of **Widget**, which is placed in *Widget.h*, is:

```
class Widget
{

public:
    // constructor and destructor
    Widget(char *name, int p);
    ~Widget();

private:
    char *myName;     // Widget's name
    int myPrice;      // and its price

};
```

The implementation in *Widget.C* is straightforward. The constructor allocates memory for the name of the widget and copies the name and price to private variables. The destructor deletes the memory allocated by the constructor:

```
Widget::Widget(char *name, int p)
{
    myName = new char[strlen(name) + 1];
    strcpy(myName, name);
    myPrice = p;
}

Widget::~Widget()
{
    delete [] myName;
}
```

Suppose we now wish to keep track of how many widgets are used in a program. How would you do it in C? Probably, you would set up a static or global variable and put an increment statement in the code everywhere you declare a **Widget**. Ugh! That's an ugly, error-prone solution.

In C++, we simply modify the class definition to include a static variable which holds a counter. If we make the counter private, we can also include a public method which returns the value of the counter:

```
class Widget {

public:
    // constructor and destructor
    Widget(char *name, int p);
    ~Widget();

    static int Num();    // returns reference count
private:
    char *myName;    // Widget's name
    int myPrice;     // and its price

    static int NumWidgets;    // reference counter

};
```

The following code is placed in *Widget.C*, along with the constructor and destructor codes:

```
// initialize the static reference counter
int Widget::NumWidgets = 0;


// define the static function
int Widget::Num()
{
    return NumWidgets;
}
```

We must make one other modification: the widget reference count must be incremented inside the **Widget** constructor. We don't need to search the code for every declaration of **Widget**, because we know that each declaration calls the constructor!

```
Widget::Widget(char *name, int p)
{
    myName = new char[strlen(name) + 1];
    strcpy(myName, name);
    myPrice = p;

    NumWidgets += 1;    // increment reference count
}
```

Now the **Widget** class can be used exactly as before in application programs, but with the additional feature of retrieving the number of widgets without requiring any other code changes:

```
// use some Widgets
for (int i = 0; i < MAX; i++) {
    Widget *w = new Widget("gadget", 0);
    // ...
    delete w;
}


// print out the total number
cout << "Number of Widgets used = "
     << Widget::Num()
     << endl;
```

Summary

In this chapter, we discussed the meaning and use of the **static** keyword inside class declarations. We described static variable and member functions and presented an example class that used static members to implement reference counting.

CHAPTER 22

TEMPLATES

She may very well pass for forty-three,
In the dusk with the light behind her.
Trial by Jury

Classes and class inheritance are a fantastic way to gain productivity through code reuse. However, they are not the only mechanism C++ provides for this purpose. Later versions of C++ compilers support the notion of **template** classes. Templates allow you to construct generic classes which can be used in an application. These templates can be declared by the application developer to operate on any type of data, and the author of the template itself does not have to know the data type.

An Example

Let's introduce templates with an example. There are many examples we could choose: binary trees, collections or sets, linked lists, etc. However, arrays of objects are familiar to every programmer, so we will create an **Array** template.

Begin by considering why an array is a generic concept. Arrays can be used to represent any linear list of elements. The data type of the element is immaterial, but for this example, all elements will be of the same type. Arrays have some general properties, such as a size, or number of elements, and each element is generally accessed using a subscript (the standard [] notation in C and C++).

A template class is declared just as any other C++ class, with the only difference being the use of **template <class T>** before the class keyword:

```
template <class T>
class Array
{

public:
    // constructor and destructor
    Array(int size);
    ~Array();
```

```
private:
    int mySize;
    T *myData;

};
```

Note that there is a constructor and destructor, a private data member that holds the size of the array, and another data member, declared as a pointer to type T. This T is the same one declared in the **template <class T>** designation in the class declaration. T is the data type that represents each element of the array. We will see later how the application actually specifies the data type when **Array** objects are declared. For now, just recognize that T is an unspecified type that we treat as any other object type (such as **int** or **char**). As the designer of the template class, we do not need to know the type to write the class.

To make the class more useful, we will write our array template so it implements bounds checking. Making sure array indices do not exceed the array boundaries is not a built-in feature of C or C++. But we can add this feature easily by overloading operator[] for the array class. This operator will take an integer argument which specifies the index of the array element desired and returns the value of the element at that index. Thus, the return type for operator[] is declared to be of type T. Here is the complete class declaration:

```
template <class T>
class Array
{

public:
    // constructor and destructor
    Array(int size);
    ~Array();

    // [] operator does bounds checking on the array
    T operator[](int index);
private:
    int mySize;
    T *myData;

};
```

Now let's write the implementation for each method. We see that the **template <class T>** designation must precede the class method name in the source code for each template class method. The other piece of odd syntax needed in the method definition is <T>, which is appended to the class name just before the scope resolution operator. This denotes that the method name is a member function of the template class which uses the T data type. Our constructor allocates memory for the array by calling the new operator to create objects of type T:

```
template <class T>
Array<T>::Array(int size)
{
    mySize = size;
    myData = new T[size];
}
```

The destructor simply deletes the memory allocated by the constructor. As we don't know the data type for the array **myData**, the **delete []** operator is used to make sure the destructor for each array element is called:

```
template <class T>
Array<T>::~Array()
{
    delete [] myData;
}
```

Our template class is completed by writing the operator[] method. Although the syntax for this method looks formidable, we are really just overloading operator[] for a template class that uses data type T. The operator takes an integer index as an argument and returns the value of the array element at that index. We do not know the actual data type, which will be determined when instances of the template class are declared, so we just use T as the return type:

```
template <class T>
T Array<T>::operator[](int index)
{
    if ((index < 0) || (index >= mySize))
        return 0;                    // error! invalid index
    else
        return myData[index];    // ok! return the value
}
```

This operator implements simple bounds checking. If the specified index to an instance of **Array** is out of bounds, the return value is zero. Otherwise, the value of the element is returned. Beware that this example only works for data types where 0 is a legal value (i.e., 0 can be cast to data type T). In a real implementation, we would probably use an **assert()** statement, throw an exception, or somehow indicate that the array bounds were exceeded.

Using the Array Template

We can now use our array class in an application. We declare arrays just as any other object, except that the data type of each array element is specified by appending the data type, enclosed in angle brackets, to the class name. Thus, an array of 1000 floats is declared as

```
Array<float> x(1000);        // array of 1000 floats
```

We can also declare arrays of any other valid type or class:

```
Array<Complex> c(10);        // 10 complex numbers
Array<String> messages(30);  // 30 Strings
Array<Dolphin> pod(150);     // 150 Dolphins
```

The overloading of **operator[]** implements bounds checking on the arrays at run time. Thus, the following code will continue to execute normally, even though the array index goes outside the bounds of the array:

```
int i, a;
Array<int> v(10);    // valid array indexes are 0..9

for (i = 0; i < 100; i++)
{
     a = v[i];    // calls operator[] for Array and
                  // returns myData[i] (or 0 if the
                  // index is invalid)
}
```

Not all compilers support templates, so make sure the compilers for your target platforms handle templates. Also note that template code may need to be compiled with special options to be used by applications. The compiler needs access to the template method implementations so code can be generated for each type of template object.

One easy way to handle template code is to place all of the template method implementations in the same header file as the template class declaration. Then only the header file needs to be included in an application that uses the template. The disadvantage of this approach is that your template source code is no longer hidden. Be sure to read the manual for your system's compiler to declare, compile, and link template code properly for applications.

Summary

In this chapter, we introduced the notion of generalized classes to facilitate the design and reuse of generic computer science and application concepts. We presented an example template class for array handling and illustrated its use in an application with several different data types.

CHAPTER 23

MULTIPLE INHERITANCE

O bitter is my cup, However could I do it.
I mixed those children up! And not a creature knew it.
HMS Pinafore

In previous chapters, you have seen many examples of how to derive a new class
from a base class. In languages such as Smalltalk, single inheritance is the only
type of derivation allowed from a base class. With C++, derived classes can
inherit from more than one base class. The ability to inherit from several different
classes simultaneously is called *multiple inheritance*. In this chapter, we will
explore multiple inheritance and present some issues related to its use.

First, when is multiple inheritance used? That's a good question, because we
already said that Smalltalk, a "pure" object-oriented language, doesn't even allow
multiple inheritance. We've already seen one example of multiple inheritance in
the iostream classes. An **iostream** behaves as both an **istream** and an **ostream**.

In general, a derived class should multiply inherit from more than one base
class whenever there is an IS-A relationship between the derived class and each of
its base classes. For example, a **Seaplane** class might inherit from both an
AirVehicle class and a **SeaVehicle** class. A **Seaplane** IS-A **AirVehicle** and a
Seaplane IS-A **SeaVehicle** (Figure 1).

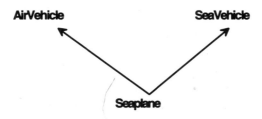

Figure 1. Class hierarchy for **Seaplane**

To declare **Seaplane** as a derived class of the existing base classes **AirVehicle** and **SeaVehicle**, use the following syntax:

```
class Seaplane : public AirVehicle, public SeaVehicle
{
        // ...
};
```

If you like, you can substitute IS-A for the colon and AND-A for the comma, so the above declaration reads "class SeaPlane IS-A AirVehicle AND-A SeaVehicle." If you read your class declarations this way, the sentence should make logical sense. Otherwise, you've probably not designed your class hierarchy properly.

There is no limit imposed by the language on the number of base classes. However, each base class is separated by a comma and includes its own access specifier (public, protected, or private).

Of course, the derived class inherits all the public and protected variables and methods from each of the base classes. This raises some interesting questions.

Duplicate Methods

Suppose **AirVehicle** and **SeaVehicle** both define a **move()** function. Which function will an instance of **Seaplane** call?

```
class AirVehicle
{
public:
    virtual void move() { cout << "I'm flying"; }
};

class SeaVehicle
{
public:
    virtual void move() { cout << "I'm floating"; }
};

class Seaplane : public AirVehicle, public SeaVehicle
{
    // ...
};

Seaplane s;
s.move();    // ERROR!  cannot resolve function to call
```

The above example will not run, because the system cannot resolve which of the methods to call. However, we can explicitly specify which function we want this way:

```
Seaplane s;
s.SeaVehicle::move();     // OK!  no ambiguity now
s.AirVehicle::move();
```

We can also do an end run around the problem by defining a **move()** function for **Seaplane** and letting that function call one or both of the inherited **move()** methods internally:

```
class Seaplane : public AirVehicle, public SeaVehicle
{
    void move();
};

void Seaplane::move()
{
    SeaVehicle::move();
    AirVehicle::move();
}

Seaplane s;
s.move();     // OK!
```

Complex Hierarchies -- A Royal Pain

Class design is more art than science, and sometimes a class designer does not foresee how the class will be used in future derived classes. This is particularly apparent with some cases of multiple inheritance. Consider the class hierarchy in Figure 2, which defines some classifications of animals.

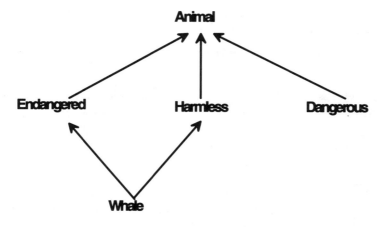

Figure 2. An animal class hierarchy

Let's suppose **Animal** contains an instance variable called **diet**. As **Whale** multiply inherits from both **Endangered** and **Harmless**, which are both derived from **Animal**, **Whale** gets two versions of **diet**! This is not what we want (it's a fluke). To ensure that only one copy of the **Animal** variables and member functions are inherited by **Whale**, it should inherit from its two base classes using the **virtual** keyword:

```
class Whale : virtual public Endangered,
              virtual public Harmless
{
    // ...
};
```

Now instances of **Whale** will have a single copy of **Animal** and thus a single copy of the instance variable **diet**. Also note that the order of the keywords **virtual** and **public** in the inheritance list is not significant. There is also no significance to the ordering of the base classes. We can also write

```
class Whale : public virtual Harmless,
              virtual public Endangered
{
    // ...
};
```

A Caveat

Considering the problems that can arise with multiple inheritance, it is no wonder there is some controversy about whether it's even a good idea. Our answer is to use multiple inheritance when

1. it makes sense for the problem,

2. it does not introduce many complexities for future derived classes, and

3. is the only option.

It is sometimes possible to redefine the class hierarchy or view the objects in a problem from more than one perspective. If an alternate view creates a class hierarchy that does not require multiple inheritance, think about using that one instead.

Summary

In this chapter, we elaborated on the concept of base and derived classes, introducing the concept of inheriting from more than one base class. We presented some issues that must be considered when designing and using multiple inheritance hierarchies.

You have now reached the end of the "jump start" section of our book. If you have read through this section and written some of the programs, you have some moderate C++ experience. When you are ready to study some more advanced examples, we have provided several self-contained chapters on advanced topics in the last part of this book.

CHAPTER 24

GUIDELINES FOR C++ PROGRAMMING

Be careful to be guided by this golden rule--
Stick close to your desks and never go to sea,
And you all may be rulers of the Queen's Navee!
HMS Pinafore

This chapter presents a list of guidelines you can follow to help better structure your C++ classes and programs. These recommendations also show some problem areas and how to avoid them. We divide these guidelines into several areas: comments, constants, classes, inheritance, and miscellaneous topics. Additional information on performance relative to C++ programs is also presented.

C++ Comments

- Avoid the use of the C++ double slash comment on the same line as a **#define** statement. If you must put comments at the end of a **#define**, use the C style comment block (/* ... */).

In the example below, some preprocessors will substitute the // comment for the **OS2** token, rather than simply defining the token. Use the second form instead:

```
#define OS2    // compiling under OS/2
#define OS2    /* compiling under OS/2 */
```

- Do not use an asterisk character immediately after the // comment. Some preprocessors confuse //* as a divide operator, followed by the start of a C style comment block, even though this is contrary to the C++ specification.

For example, the following code may be incorrectly parsed as **x=a/b;** instead of **x=a**:

```
x = a//* b is usually equal to 10 */b;
```

Constants

- The **const** keyword is preferred over **#define** in defining constants for use in a program. Variables declared as **const** are type-checked by the compiler. The following example shows a definition that should be replaced with a **const** variable:

```
#define WM_PAINT 0x2000
const long WM_PAINT = 0x2000;
```

- Use enumerated types in place of a series of **#defines**. The set of file errors below can be replaced with an enumerated type, **FileError**:

```
#define FILE_OK          0
#define FILE_NOT_FOUND   1
#define FILE_READ_ERROR  2
#define FILE_WRITE_ERROR 3

// replace the above definitions with an enum type
enum FileError
{
        FILE_OK,
        FILE_NOT_FOUND,
        FILE_READ_ERROR,
        FILE_WRITE_ERROR
};
```

Class Structures

- A common convention is to list friends of a class first followed by the public members of a class in the class definition. Follow the public members by protected members, with private members listed last. When you look at the class definition, you should first see the public and protected interfaces, which should be the only part of concern to you as a class user.
- It is useful to place the declaration of a class into a header file and the implementation of the class methods in a separate source file. This facilitates distribution of classes by simply publishing the class header file and the object module containing the compiled source code for the methods.
- Each class should get its own header and source file. The header file should contain a conditional **#define** to avoid including the class definition more than once anywhere the header file is used.

For example, for a class named **Seaplane**, the *Seaplane.h* file should contain the following (or similar) definitions:

```
#ifndef MODULE_Seaplaneh
#define MODULE_Seaplaneh

    // put class declaration here

#endif
```

- Each class represents an object type which may fail to initialize when its constructor or an internal class method called by the constructor fails. If you define an internal error variable for each class, you can use this to check that the object variables have valid values before carrying out operations that may depend on these values. In addition, constructors cannot return any values, so providing a function to check whether a constructor initialized an object properly is a good idea. Alternatively, you can use C++ exceptions for this purpose, but only a few compilers support exceptions at this time.

Inheritance

- The header files for base classes should be included by the header file of the derived class. Then, the application modules that use the derived class declaration and source module only need to include the derived class header file. The base class files will be included automatically by the derived class header, and the **#define** wrapper in the base class header files will prevent the class declarations from occurring more than once.
- Destructors should almost always be declared virtual. This ensures that the order of the destructors for the derived and base classes are always called in the proper order.
- Although somewhat controversial, some C++ authors recommend declaring all public and protected members of a class as virtual. This is consistent with Smalltalk, where all object types are resolved at run time. Users of any C++ derived classes which override virtual base class methods will then call the correct method. This may have performance implications on some systems, so we feel no hard-and-fast rule is appropriate.
- If you overload the **new** operator for a class, never declare it virtual. Programmers who derive classes from a base class with an overloaded virtual **new** method may be surprised when the use of **new** in the derived class does not perform as expected.

- Private methods of a class should never be declared virtual. These methods cannot be called by either derived classes or outside functions anyway (with the exception of friend functions or friend classes).
- The protected attribute is not always necessary. A class designer can declare all variables private and provide get and set methods for the variables as appropriate.
- Try to minimize your use of multiple inheritance. Only use this concept if your application domain requires it, and you cannot redefine the class hierarchy to require only single inheritance.

Miscellaneous

- Instead of propagating a lot of get and set member functions throughout your code (**GetValue()**, **SetValue()**, **GetX()**, **SetX()**, etc.), use function overloading. Define get and set methods with the same function name. The context and argument list of the method denote whether it is getting or setting a value:

```
int Value() const;    // get function
void Value(int v);    // set function
```

- Use **inline** functions in place of macros, and only declare simple member functions as inline. Also, put the inline definitions for member functions in the class header file, rather than in the same source file as the other member functions. Some programmers place their inline code in a separate *.inl* file instead.
- Use 0 rather than NULL in C++ programs. Some compilers define NULL as (void *)0. Using 0 for NULL pointer values is guaranteed to be type-safe in C++.
- Minimize your use of **friend** classes and functions. Friend designations override the encapsulation of the class and can usually be eliminated by using protected variables. If not, examine your class hierarchy to see if a change is warranted so friend declarations are not needed.

Performance Issues

No one would claim that compilers are great examples of artificial intelligence, but the optimizations done by compilers today are quite sophisticated. In most cases, the compiler can optimize code faster than it takes you to think of clever coding tricks to enhance performance. It pays to put your initial coding effort into getting the program running, and running correctly.

After all, if you have trouble getting a program running when you are coding an algorithm straightforwardly, you will have almost no chance of coding a version which uses clever optimizations to perform faster.

If an optimizing compiler cannot speed up your program sufficiently, try estimating or using a profiling tool to determine where the program needs performance tuning. Then rewrite only that section of code. Trying to squeeze the last ounce of performance from every line of code you write decreases your productivity, increases the likelihood the program will not be correct, and creates a maintenance headache (or nightmare).

Given the above, there are a few things to keep in mind when coding C++ applications:

- Use short inline functions where possible.
- If you are sure a class will not be used as a base class for future derived classes, eliminate all virtual function declarations in the class.
- Do not declare variables until they are needed. Constructors which get called when variables are declared can sometimes do a lot of initialization work. By declaring all variables at the top of a function, all of their constructor work gets done whether the function actually uses the variable or not.
- Use an optimizing compiler and a profiling tool. Remember the 80:20 rule: 80% of the work is done by 20% of the code.
- Find a better algorithm!

Remember -- performance only matters when it isn't good enough.

Exercises

The following exercises may help you understand how you might use C++ to solve real programming problems:

1. A vehicle is on the beach, *b* miles from a road. The road runs parallel to the beach. A hot dog stand is *h* miles down the road. The vehicle can travel 20 mph along the beach and 45 mph along the road. For various values of *b* and *h*, compute the shortest travelling angle from the beach to the hot dog stand.

2. A well-known liberal arts college holds student government elections using a proportional redistribution system of votes. Students vote for their first through fifth choices for student representatives. The votes are tallied so that each candidate receives 100% of the first place votes, 80% of the second place votes, 60% of the third place votes, etc. Write a program to find the winners among 10 candidates from a file of 30 lines

by 10 columns, where each column contains 0 (for no vote) through 5 (for fifth place vote).

3. Write a program to count the frequency of alphabetic characters irrespective of case in a manuscript.

4. Write a program to search for all occurrences of a specified string in a document and replace them with a new specified string.

5. A small prep school uses a "raffle system" at tables of 10 people to distribute second helpings of food. Any person may request a raffle if more people want seconds than are available on the plate. Each student holds up 0 to 5 fingers which are added into a total. The person conducting the raffle counts around the table clockwise that many places to find where the platter starts. It is then passed to the right (counterclockwise). Compute the results of several hypothetical raffles, and if there are three second helpings available, compute the optimum number of fingers to hold up if you are conducting the raffle. Use a random number generator.

Summary

We have presented some recommendations for structuring your C++ programs. We listed problems we have encountered and some things you should try to avoid. We also discussed performance issues and approaches for increasing application speed.

ADVANCED C++ EXAMPLES

CHAPTER 25

EXCEPTIONS

The thing is really quite simple -- the insertion of a single word will do it. Let it stand that every fairy shall die who <u>don't</u> marry a mortal , and there you are, out of your difficulty at once!
Iolanthe

Exceptions are defined as errors which generally cause a program to fail, or terminate, unexpectedly. These can be errors such as divide by zero, out of memory, resources exhausted, array bounds exceeded, etc.

Under C, exceptions are typically handled by signals. Some operating systems define their own exception-handling mechanism, which either works in conjunction with or maps directly to signal handlers. C++ adds its own exception handling independent of either the operating system or C signals. This chapter covers some basics of C++ exceptions.

Handling Errors

Suppose we have a class, say **Vector**, which allocates space for an array of numbers:

```
class Vector
{

public:

    Vector(int size);
    ~Vector();

private:

    int mySize;        // size of array
    double *myArray;   // pointer to memory
};
```

The constructor saves the requested size and allocates the memory, while the destructor deallocates the array:

```
Vector::Vector(int size)
{
   mySize = size;
   myArray = new double[mySize];
}

Vector::~Vector()
{
   delete [] myArray;
}
```

So far, we haven't added any error checking to our example. For instance, what happens when the **new** operator fails and returns 0 because no more memory is available? A lot of our examples have glossed over this point up to now. Programmers all have their own techniques for dealing with this situation.

One method for handling the error is just to print an error message and end the program:

```
myArray = new double[mySize];

if (!myArray) {
   cerr << "No more memory!";
   abort();
}
```

Of course, this may or may not be acceptable to a user, who should rightfully expect a more graceful recovery from such an error.

A second method could set an internal error flag for the class and provide a method to return the status. This is very common for catching errors that occur inside a constructor, because a constructor cannot return a value denoting success or failure. Using this technique, the **Vector** class declaration becomes

```
enum state { NO_ERROR, MEMORY_ERROR };

class Vector
{
public:

   Vector(int size);
   ~Vector();

   inline state Error() const { return myError; }

private:

   int mySize;          // size of array
   double *myArray;     // pointer to memory

   state myError;       // current state
};
```

The constructor now sets the state of the object using one of the enumerated values declared above:

```
Vector::Vector(int size)
{
   mySize = size;
   myArray = new double[mySize];

   if (!myArray)
      myError = MEMORY_ERROR;
   else
      myError = NO_ERROR;
}
```

Any code that creates an instance of the **Vector** class can now check the error code:

```
Vector v1(100);
if (v1.Error() == MEMORY_ERROR) {
       // put code to handle error here
}
```

C++ Exception Handling

The last example illustrates how errors that happen in a class constructor can be handled, but the burden is on the user of the class to call the error method. C++ allows a standard implementation for error handling to be defined, known as **throw**ing an exception. An exception effectively transfers control from the point where the exception occurred to an exception handler.

Exception Handlers

An exception handler is usually defined as a class. In our **Vector** example, we can define a handler for memory errors. This particular handler simply prints a message and exits the program. In this case, we've shown the handler constructor with two arguments, which are used to form a more informative message to indicate exactly where the exception occurred:

```
class MemoryAllocation
{

public:
   MemoryAllocation(char *arg, char *name)
   {
      cerr << "Error allocating memory for "
            << arg
            << " in the class named "
            << name
            << endl;
      exit(1);
```

```
    }
};
```

Of course, the exception handler is just a class, so it may contain other member functions and variables as well.

The try Block and catch Statement

To use the exception handler in our **Vector** class constructor, we enclose the operation inside a **try** block. For each exception we want to process inside the **try** block, we also provide a **catch** statement. Each **catch** statement is the point at which execution will resume when a **throw** statement is executed:

```
Vector::Vector(int size)
{
    mySize = size;

    try {
        // this is the try block
        myArray = new double[mySize];

        if (!myArray)
            throw MemoryAllocation("myArray", "Vector");
    }
    // the catch statement(s) go here
    catch (MemoryAllocation) {}
}
```

Now when the new operator fails to allocate memory, the constructor throws a **MemoryAllocation** object, which prints the following message and ends the program:

```
Error allocating memory for myArray in the class named Vector.
```

If we had wanted the program to continue, we could have left the **exit()** statement out of the **MemoryAllocation** constructor. The exception would still be thrown and the message would be printed out, but the program would resume execution. However, execution does not resume at the same point the exception occurred, but resumes at the **catch** statement after the closing brace of the **try** block. In this case, there are no more executable statements after the **try** block, so control returns to the point in the program where the constructor was called.

Adding catch Handlers

Of course, you can have many **try** blocks and multiple **catch** statements. Let's add another type of exception that is raised whenever the size argument passed to the

Vector constructor is zero or negative. Start by declaring an exception handler class named **IllegalArgument,** which prints out what variable name was passed with an illegal value and to which function the value was passed:

```
class IllegalArgument
{
public:
    IllegalArgument(char *arg, char *name)
    {
        cerr << "An illegal value for "
            << arg
            << " was passed to "
            << name
            << endl;
        exit(1);
    }
};
```

Now we enclose the assignment statement for checking the **size** argument in the **try** block, and add another **catch** statement for the new exception type:

```
Vector::Vector(int size)
{
    // initialize the private variables
    mySize = 0;
    myArray = 0;

    try {
        // check the input argument
        if (size <= 0)
            throw IllegalArgument("size",
                                "Vector::Vector");

        // allocate the memory
        mySize = size;
        myArray = new double[mySize];

        if (!myArray)
            throw MemoryAllocation("myArray", "Vector");
    }

    catch (IllegalArgument) {}
    catch (MemoryAllocation) {}
}
```

You can also put other code in the braces following each catch handler statement, and this code will be executed after the code in the exception class has completed.

Exception Support

Not all compiler vendors include support for C++ exception handling. However, the C++ exception-handling mechanism is gaining acceptance with developers. By the time this book is published, more than half of the C++ compiler vendors will provide support for C++ exceptions. You should check for exception support on the particular compilers and operating systems you target for applications and libraries.

Summary

We introduced the notion of exception handling in C++. Examples illustrated how exceptions are defined and how they effect program execution. We also briefly discussed compiler support for C++ exception handling.

mkclass

Don't say that your honour -- love levels all ranks.
It does to a considerable extent, but it does not level them as much as that.
HMS Pinafore

We have included a utility program with this book to help you generate your own C++ classes. A quick glance at the example class declarations throughout this book will show that each class contains a lot of boilerplate code. Most classes have a public interface and a private section. Most also include both a constructor and a destructor, along with an include directive in the class source module for the header file containing the class declaration.

It is also a good idea to include declarations in your classes for both the copy constructor and **operator=** methods. If you then accidentally use a copy constructor or **operator=** in the code which uses the class, a compiler error will warn you that the method is not yet defined. Coplien[1] also recommends including these declarations as part of his canonical form.

As class creation is a frequent activity in writing C++ programs, we wrote **mkclass** as a command line utility to standardize and simplify the generation of C++ class declaration and source code modules. You are free to copy and reuse the **mkclass** code presented below and modify and compile it for your favorite operating system. The code has been successfully compiled for DOS, OS/2, AIX, UNIX, and Windows NT.

The source code for **mkclass** is a main program module, *mkclass.C*, and two additional classes, **CPPFile** and **CmdLine**. **CPPFile** actually generates the source code header file and source module based on parameters supplied on the command line. **CmdLine** is a general class for parsing and reporting the options supplied on the command line for the program. You can enhance the **CmdLine** class or use it unchanged for handling the command line in your own applications.

Using mkclass

Once you have compiled and linked **mkclass** on your system, you can start the program by typing

```
mkclass
```

  or

```
mkclass -?
```

which will display the program title, version, and valid command line flags and arguments.

To generate a class, say **Editor**, as a base class, use the following syntax:

```
mkclass -c Editor
```

This will generate two files: *Editor.h*, the header file containing the class declaration, and *Editor.C*, the source code module containing code stubs for the constructor and destructor declared in *Editor.h*.

You can also generate new classes that are derived from one, two, or three base classes, using the b1, b2, and b3 flags. For instance, generate a class called **EditWindow**, which inherits from both **Editor** and another class called **Window**:

```
mkclass -c EditWindow -b1 Editor -b2 Window
```

This command generates *EditWindow.h* and *EditWindow.C*, defining **EditWindow** as inheriting from **Editor** and **Window** and including the constructor calls to **Editor** and **Window** in the constructor code stub. One problem is that some file systems do not allow more than eight characters for a base filename. The "f" flag handles this by letting you specify an alternate filename that is not based on the class name.

```
mkclass -c EditWindow -b1 Editor -b2 Window -f editwin
```

This command generates the same code as before, but the header and source code are stored in *editwin.h* and *editwin.C*. If you prefer your C++ code modules to be named with a *.cpp* extension instead, use the "e" option:

```
mkclass -c EditWindow -b1 Editor -b2 Window -f editwin
 -e cpp
```

As you saw in the chapter on templates, the declaration syntax for C++ templates can be difficult to remember. The "t" flag causes **mkclass** to generate the class declaration and source code method stubs which include the template syntax automatically. Just include the flag along with any other flags on the command line:

```
mkclass -c LinkedList -f linklist -t
```

If you look at the code modules created by **mkclass**, you will see a standard comment block at the top of each module, along with some simple, automatically generated comments about the class. Almost every programmer, group, company, and organization defines its own standards for code headers. Thus, we have included an "h" flag, which can specify the filename of a text file containing your own replacement comment block. For example, if your company header comment block is in a file called *copyrite.txt*, the text in this file overwrites the standard comment block:

```
mkclass -c Pawn -h copyrite.txt
```

Example Output

Here is a sample header file created by **mkclass**, using the following command:

```
mkclass -c Pawn -b1 ChessPiece
```

This command creates the file *Pawn.h*, containing a new class declaration for **Pawn**, which is derived from the **ChessPiece** class.

```
// ********************************************************
//
// Module:   Pawn.h
// Author:
//
// Purpose: C++ class header file for Pawn
//
// Notes:   This class is derived from ChessPiece.
//
// ********************************************************

#ifndef MODULE_Pawnh
#define MODULE_Pawnh

#include "ChessPiece.h"

// constants and internal data types for class
const int PawnMajorVersion = 1;
```

```
const int PawnMinorVersion = 0;

// error types
enum {
    Pawn_NO_ERROR
};

// class declaration
class Pawn : public ChessPiece {

public:

    // constructor and destructor
    Pawn();
    virtual ~Pawn();

    // get error value
    inline long Error() { return myError; }

private:

    long myError;           // error value

    // private copy constructor and operator= (define these
    // and make them public to enable copy and assignment
    // of the class)
    Pawn(const Pawn&);
    Pawn& operator=(const Pawn&);

};

#endif

// ************************************************************

// end of Pawn.h
```

Notice that after the standard comment block, the entire class declaration is enclosed in a **#ifndef/#endif** wrapper, as we noted in Chapter 13. This prevents the class declaration from being repeated if included more than once in another module. In addition to declaring a constructor and virtual destructor, the program generates private declarations of the copy constructor and operator= methods. Also, constants are declared to hold the version number for the class, and an enumerated type is used to maintain and return the error state for any object of the class.

The *Pawn.C* file created from the above command includes the standard comment block and code stubs for the constructor and destructor. Note that the derived class constructor also includes a call to the base class constructor:

```
// ************************************************************
//
// Module:  Pawn.C
```

```
// Author:
//
// Purpose: C++ class source file for Pawn
//
// Notes:  This class is derived from ChessPiece.
//
// ********************************************************

#include "Pawn.h"

// ********************************************************

// Pawn - constructor

Pawn::Pawn()
    : ChessPiece()

{
    // init instance variables
    myError = Pawn_NO_ERROR;
}

// ---------------------------------------------------------

// ~Pawn - destructor

Pawn::~Pawn()

{
}

// ********************************************************

// end of Pawn.C
```

Once **mkclass** generates the files, they may be compiled right away.

The Main Program

This section discusses how the **mkclass** program is structured. Refer to the source code included on the diskette that came with this book when reading this discussion.

The **mkclass** program consists of a main routine, some nonmember functions, and two classes. The main program in *mkclass.C* first prints the title and current version number of the program. An instance of the **CmdLine** class is then created using the **argc** and **argv** arguments supplied to **main()**.

CmdLine

The constructor of **CmdLine** sets an internal error flag that is checked by calling the **CmdLine::Error()** function. If the **CmdLine** object was created with no errors and there is at least one argument in the command line (i.e., the program name), determined by a call to **CmdLine::NumArguments()**, the program continues. Otherwise, some help information is displayed and the program exits.

Next, all of the valid command line flags that can be specified by the user are registered using the **CmdLine::Flag()** method. Each call to **Flag()** takes either one or two arguments. One argument signifies that the flag character or flag string is just a toggle on the command line, which turns that particular feature on or off. Two arguments specify that the user must supply a value for the flag. The data type of the value is specified in the second argument to **Flag()** as being a string, integer, or floating point number.

For example, the **mkclass** source code registers "c" as a flag which requires a string argument, which will be the name of the class generated. "t" is registered as a flag with no arguments and denotes that a template class should be generated whenever a -t toggle argument appears in the command line:

```
void register_flags(CmdLine& cl)
{
    // the -c flag requires a string argument
    cl.Flag("c", CMDLINE_STRING);

    // the -t flag is an on/off toggle
    cl.Flag("t");
}
```

Once the valid flags and their arguments are registered, **mkclass** calls some **CmdLine** methods to make sure all flags specified by the user are valid and that the required flag "c" which specifies the class name is present.

CPPFile

If the command line arguments are valid, the nonmember function **process_request()** in *mkclass.C* is called. Inside **process_request()**, the base class name and source code file extension are retrieved from the **CmdLine** object.

An instance of **CPPFile**, the object that actually generates the code, is then created. A switch statement detects whether the instance is generated without error by calling the object's public **Error()** method. A loop queries the **CmdLine** object to see if any base classes need to be registered with the **CPPFile** object using the **CPPFile::AddBase()** method. The base names are extracted from the command line as the string arguments to the b1, b2, and b3 flags. Finally, the **CPPFile::WriteHeader()** and **CPPFile::WriteSource()** functions are called to generate the output files.

You may want to spend some time studying the internals of **CmdLine** and **CPPFile** to see how these objects maintain and use their private variables, allocate and deallocate memory, and use the iostream methods for file I/O. You may also find ways to improve the interface and implementation. For example, **CPPFile** might be improved by deriving classes for the source and header file code generation, rather than including these in one class. It is important for you to experiment with working programs to appreciate the design and complexity trade-offs the author made and to gain insight on techniques you can incorporate in your own programs.

Exercises

1. Add an "a" flag to the program to specify the last name of the author of a class. Change the output files so this name is included in the standard comment block of the output files. What changes must be made to **CmdLine** to support a flag which takes a string argument that contains embedded spaces?

2. Rewrite **CPPFile** as an abstract base class. Derive the output files as separate classes from this new class.

3. Redesign the program using the object-oriented design steps presented in an earlier chapter. Implement your design.

Reference

1. J. O. Coplien, *Advanced C++ Programming Styles and Idioms*, Addison-Wesley, Reading, MA, 1992.

CHAPTER 27

A GENERIC LINKED LIST CLASS

> *As someday it may happen that a victim must be found, I've got a little list. I've got a little list.*
> **The Mikado**

Linked lists are one of the most useful generic computing concepts. They can be used to represent sparse arrays or matrices in mathematical algorithms, cells in a spreadsheet, sequences of graphics commands stored in a metafile, lists of open windows in a graphical user interface, etc. The advantages of linked lists over arrays are more efficient use of memory and ease of inserting or removing elements inside the list without shifting large blocks of memory.

Almost every C++ library seems to include one or more classes that deal exclusively with constructing, maintaining and traversing linked lists. Because linked lists are so common in many programs, their implementation using C++ templates provides an interesting example to study and shows the power of C++ relative to ANSI C. In addition, you can use the code in this chapter unchanged or modify it for use in your own programs.

Definitions and Terminology

We first need to set up some common terminology for discussing our linked list implementation. A linked list is simply a linear chain of elements, or nodes. Each node is typically represented by a C structure or C++ class. One node, called the head, is the first element in the list. As shown in Figure 1, each node contains a pointer to the next list entry. Such a list is called a singly linked list. If each node also contains a pointer to the previous element in the list, the list is a doubly linked list.

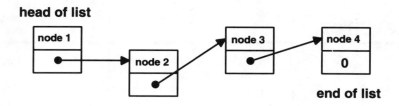

Figure 1. A visual representation of a singly linked list

It is useful to refer to diagrams such as Figure 1 to visualize how to traverse a list using a loop or how to update the node pointers in order to add or delete list elements. Note that the last node has a 0 (NULL) pointer to indicate that there are no more elements in the list.

Implementing a Linked List Node

Each node in the list contains information about that particular list element. As shown in the diagram, each node must also contain a pointer to another structure or class of the same type. We can represent this type of structure easily in either C or C++.

Let's say we wish to store spreadsheet data as a linked list of cells. Thus, each cell needs an integer row and character column designation, along with one or more variable types representing the cell data. In this example, we will limit the cell data types to a floating point value or a text string that fits in 80 characters (including a terminating NULL character):

```
struct Cell
{
    int row;          /* row and column of cell */
    char column;
    double value;     /* floating point value */
    char text[80];    /* text string */
};
```

The C Approach

In C, we can define a new structure called **Node** as follows:

```
struct Node
{
    struct Cell scell;   /* data for this element */
    struct Node *next;   /* pointer to next element */
};
```

Now all variables of type **Node** can be valid elements of a linked list of nodes. Alternatively, we can modify the original definition of **Cell** to include a pointer to the next cell:

```
struct Cell
{
    int row;                /* row and column of cell */
    char column;
    double value;           /* floating point value */
    char text[80];          /* text string */
    struct Cell *next;      /* pointer to next element */
};
```

This cell data type can now be used directly as a linked list element, but we have introduced a maintenance problem in the program, because a structure definition has changed.

In both cases, we are adding a new property, or variable, to an existing data type. The new property is a pointer that allows the data type to be used as a linked list element. This is a great place to use a C++ template.

A C++ Template for Nodes

Let's define a C++ template called **LinkedListElement**, which is defined to hold a pointer to an instance of any data type:

```
template <class T>
class LinkedListElement
{

public:

    // constructor and destructor
    LinkedListElement(T *entry);
    virtual ~LinkedListElement() {}

private:

    T *myEntry;    // pointer to instance of data type

    // previous and next list elements
    LinkedListElement<T> *Prev;
    LinkedListElement<T> *Next;

};
```

The constructor for our template class initializes the private variable **myEntry**, which keeps a copy of the pointer to the data for the linked list element. The **Prev** and **Next** pointers are also initialized to 0, to enable an instance of the template class to be used as an element of either a singly or a doubly linked list:

```
template <class T>
LinkedListElement<T>::LinkedListElement(T *entry)
{
    // init instance variables
    myEntry = entry;
    Prev = 0;
    Next = 0;
}
```

Now this template can be used with our original **Cell** data type, or any other data type, to automatically add previous and next pointers so the data can be added to a linked list. For example, the following allocates a new cell that can be added to a linked list:

```
// allocate memory for a new spreadsheet cell
Cell *temp = new Cell;

// declare a pointer to a linked list element that
// holds Cell data
LinkedListElement<Cell> *pelem;

// and create a new linked list element
pelem = new LinkedListElement<Cell>(temp);
```

That last statement looks confusing. All it does is allocate memory for a new **LinkedListElement**. However, **LinkedListElement** is a template, so we must specify the type of data that the template will deal with, which is a **Cell**. In addition, we supply an argument to the **LinkedListElement** constructor, which is a pointer to an instance of the **Cell** class.

Note that the original definition of **Cell** does not change -- the template instance adds the previous and next pointers that the linked list itself needs. Client code that operates only with the contents of the structure does not have access to or need to know about pointers to other cell elements.

Constructing a Linked List

If we now want to use our list node to build a linked list, we need to initialize a pointer to the head of the list to zero and store the head somewhere. In C, the head would typically be stored as a static variable in the module where the linked list operation functions are written. Client code then operates on the list through these functions.

However, this doesn't allow programming of a generic linked list interface. Each linked list element in C is a structure with a pointer to the next element, and the linked list functions must know the type of structure and the name of the next element pointer variable. Thus, for every data type where we need a linked list, we must build a new set of functions specific for that data type.

That recipe sounds like another good place to use a C++ template! We can define a generic template class called **LinkedList** which will contain all of the methods needed to access, add, and delete list elements. With this template class, you can easily implement a linked list on any data type without writing any additional code.

The LinkedList Class Declaration

Here is an initial declaration for our **LinkedList** template:

```
template <class T>
class LinkedList
{

public:

    // constructor and destructor (note that the default
    // is for the list to automatically delete the list
    // entries when the list is destroyed)
    LinkedList(int delete_entries = 1);
    virtual ~LinkedList();

    // methods to add or remove entries from the list
    int Add(const T *entry);
    int Remove(const T *entry);

    // method to remove all entries from the list
    void Purge();

    // method to retrieve items from the list
    T *Get(unsigned long index);

    // method to get the number of entries in the list
    inline unsigned long Count() const {return myCount;}

private:

    // set this flag to TRUE if entries should be
    // deleted when the list instance is deleted
    int doDeleteEntries;

    LinkedListElement<T> *myHead;    // head of list

    unsigned long myCount;    // total number of elements

    // methods to find a linked list element
    LinkedListElement<T> *FindElement(const T *entry);
    LinkedListElement<T> *FindLastElement();

};
```

This declaration defines **LinkedList** on a data type of class T, which can be any type you choose. As each element of the linked list must have a pointer to the next element, we can implement our **LinkedList** class on nodes of type **LinkedListElement**. Thus, an instance of **LinkedList<Cell>** would maintain a linked list of cells. Internally, the list actually maintains the cells as nodes with a data type of **LinkedListElement<Cell>**. As a user, you don't have to know anything about **LinkedListElement** -- your code will only operate on instances of **Cell**, and these can be added or removed from the linked list by calling the **LinkedList** template methods.

The head of the linked list is stored in the private variable **myHead**, which is a pointer to a **LinkedListElement**. There is also a private variable that stores the total number of elements in the list and an inline public method called **Count()** that returns the number of elements.

The Constructor and Destructor

Note that our constructor has a default argument, which is a flag which denotes what happens to each element of the list when that element is deleted. We need this because the list is defined to store pointers to instances of data that are added to the list. For example, we might allocate 10 cell instances and put them in a linked list this way:

```
// define a linked list of Cells and put 10 cells in
// the list, numbering the cells from A1 to A10
LinkedList<Cell> aList;

for (int i = 1; i <= 10; i++) {
    // allocate a new cell and initialize its position
    Cell *p = new Cell;
    p->row = i;
    p->column = 'A';

    aList.Add(p);    // add to the linked list
}
```

In this example, we did not keep our own copy of the pointer to each new **Cell** instance we allocated, but each pointer is stored in the linked list. So when any element of the list is destroyed, we would like the list to automatically delete the pointer to the data as well. The constructor stores the flag argument in a private variable called **doDeleteEntries**.

Here is the **LinkedList** constructor:

```
template <class T>
LinkedList<T>::LinkedList(int delete_entries)
{
```

```
    // init instance variables
    if (delete_entries)
        doDeleteEntries = 1;
    else
        doDeleteEntries = 0;

    myHead = 0;
    myCount = 0L;
}
```

In addition to initializing the delete flag, the constructor sets the list head pointer and the element count to 0.

The destructor simply calls the public method **Purge()**, which deletes all of the elements from the list before the list is destroyed:

```
template <class T>
LinkedList<T>::~LinkedList()
{
    Purge();  // removes all items from the list
}
```

The **Purge()** method is defined below. It works by deleting the head of the list, so the second element becomes the new head. This loop continues until no more elements are left:

```
template <class T>
void LinkedList<T>::Purge()
{
    // loop through the list, deleting all of the list
    // elements - if the doDeleteEntries flag was set
    // when the list was created, also delete the
    // information contained in each element
    LinkedListElement<T> *p;

    while (myHead) {
        p = myHead->Next;

        // delete the element
        if (doDeleteEntries)
            delete myHead->myEntry;
        delete myHead;

        // set up the next element to be the new head
        if (p)
            p->Prev = 0;
        myHead = p;
    }

    myCount = 0L;  // reset the count
}
```

We need to make a change in our **LinkedListElement** declaration now. We see that **Purge()** requires access to the **Prev** and **Next** pointers of

LinkedListElement and to the **myEntry** pointer of the data stored in the element. Our initial declaration of **LinkedListElement** defined these as private variables, so we need to declare **LinkedList** as a friend of **LinkedListElement** to access these variables. While we're at it, we can also declare the methods in **LinkedListElement** private, so only instances of **LinkedList** can create or access **LinkedListElements**:

```
template <class T>
class LinkedListElement
{

friend class LinkedList<T>;

private:

    // constructor and destructor
    LinkedListElement(T *entry);
    virtual ~LinkedListElement() {}

    T *myEntry;        // pointer to instance of data type

    LinkedListElement<T> *Prev;   // prev list element
    LinkedListElement<T> *Next;   // next list element

};
```

The Add Method

To add a new element to the list, we must first allocate a new **LinkedListElement** that contains a pointer to the data we want stored in the element. Then, the element is added to the end of the list. A check is made to set the head of the list to the new element if the list is empty:

```
template <class T>
int LinkedList<T>::Add(const T *entry)
{
    // allocate memory for a new list element
    LinkedListElement<T> *p;
    p = new LinkedListElement<T>(entry);
    if (!p)
        return 1;      // failed!

    // add the element to the list
    if (!myHead) {
        // no head of list - new element becomes the head
        myHead = p;
    } else {
        // find the last element in the list
        LinkedListElement<T> *last = FindLastElement();

        // set the new element's Prev pointer to point
        // to the last element and the Next pointer to 0
```

```
        p->Prev = last;
        p->Next = 0;

        // make p the new last element of the list
        last->Next = p;
    }

    myCount += 1L;    // increment the count
    return 0;         // success!
}
```

To append an item to the list, we use a method called **FindLastElement()** to return the last element in the list. Our initial class declaration includes this as a private method, and its implementation is given below. The method simply traverses the list until an entry is found with a **Next** pointer of 0, which defines the last element of the list:

```
template <class T>
LinkedListElement<T> *LinkedList<T>::FindLastElement()
{
    // look for the element with a Next pointer of 0
    LinkedListElement<T> *p = myHead;

    while (p && (p->Next != 0))
        p = p->Next;

    return p;
}
```

The Remove Method

Elements are deleted from the linked list using the **Remove()** method. **Remove()** first finds the element to be deleted and then tests whether this is the first element or another element in the list. If it is the first element, the list head pointer is updated. If the element to be removed is inside the list, the node pointers for the nodes on either side of the one being deleted are updated to point at each other before the target node is deleted:

```
template <class T>
int LinkedList<T>::Remove(const T *entry)
{
    // find the element which matches the
    // input argument
    LinkedListElement<T> *p = FindElement(entry);
    if (!p)
        return 1;      // not found!

    // remove the element
    if (p == myHead) {
        // remove the first list element by setting up
        // the second element as the new element
        myHead = p->Next;
```

```
        if (myHead)
            myHead->Prev = 0;

        // delete the element
        if (doDeleteEntries)
            delete p->myEntry;
        delete p;
    } else {
        // remove an internal list element
        LinkedListElement<T> *item1 = p->Prev;
        LinkedListElement<T> *item2 = p->Next;

        // update the node pointers for the elements on
        // either side of the one being deleted
        if (item1)
            item1->Next = item2;
        if (item2)
            item2->Prev = item1;

        // delete the element
        if (doDeleteEntries)
            delete p->myEntry;
        delete p;
    }

    myCount -= 1L;    // decrement the count
    return 0;         // success!
}
```

This method relies on another private method, **FindElement()**, that returns the **LinkedListElement** corresponding to the input pointer. **FindElement()** is implemented as a list traversal which tests if the input pointer matches the **myEntry** pointer stored inside each **LinkedListElement**. It returns a zero if no match can be found:

```
template <class T>
LinkedListElement<T> *
LinkedList<T>::FindElement(const T *entry)

{
    // look through the list for an element containing
    // the same entry pointer as the one passed to this
    // method
    LinkedListElement<T> *p = myHead;

    while (p) {
        if (p->myEntry == entry)
            return p;     // found it!

        p = p->Next;
    }

    return 0;    // not found
}
```

The Get Method

The final method in our **LinkedList** implementation is a **Get()** method, which retrieves a pointer to the data stored in a particular list element. The argument to this method is an unsigned long index, which refers to one of the list elements (starting from index 0):

```
template <class T>
T *LinkedList<T>::Get(unsigned long index)
{
    // test for no entries or illegal argument
    if ((myCount == 0L) || (index >= myCount))
        return 0;

    // look through the list for the index(th) element
    unsigned long i = 0L;
    LinkedListElement<T> *p = myHead;

    while (i < index) {
        i += 1L;
        if (p)
            p = p->Next;
    }

    // return the entry contained in this element, or
    // 0 if no element was found
    if (p)
        return p->myEntry;
    else
        return 0;
}
```

Note that **Get()** returns a pointer to an instance of data type T, not a pointer to a **LinkedListElement** (which holds the T * pointers). We don't want to require the user of the **LinkedList** class to know anything about **LinkedListElements**. The user is only concerned with pointers to the data type T. How the **LinkedList** template manages the pointers to the user data types is completely hidden.

Using LinkedList

Now that we have a complete implementation for our linked list template, we can write code to use it for constructing linked lists for any data type. Define a spreadsheet cell class as follows:

```
class Cell
{

public:

    // constructor and destructor
    Cell(int r, char c) { row = r; col = c; }
```

```
~Cell() {}

    // get and set methods for setting the value
    // of the cell
    inline void Value(double v) { myValue = v; }
    inline double Value() const { return myValue; }

    // print method for the cell
    inline void Print() { cout << myValue << endl; }
private:

    int row;          // row and column of cell
    char col;

    double myValue;   // floating point value
};
```

Now declare a spreadsheet as a linked list of spreadsheet cells and set up 10 cells from A1 to A10:

```
LinkedList<Cell> spreadsheet;

// add cells
for (int i = 1; i <= 10; i++) {
    // allocate a new cell and initialize its position
    Cell *p = new Cell(i, 'A');

    // set value to the row number
    p->Value(i);

    // add the cell to the spreadsheet
    spreadsheet.Add(p);
}
```

If you want to delete the fifth entry,

```
Cell *p = spreadsheet.Get(4);
spreadsheet.Remove(p);
```

To print the remaining values, use the **Cell::Print()** method:

```
for (int index = 0L; index < spreadsheet.Count();
     index++) {
    Cell *p = spreadsheet.Get(index);

    if (p)
        p->Print();
}
```

Suggested Exercises

1. Extend the **LinkedList** class to handle the case where the user tries to add a duplicate entry to the list.

2. Overload the **Add()** method to insert an entry anywhere in the list, rather than just appending to the list.

3. Write two new **LinkedList** methods called **First()** and **Next()** which enable the user to traverse through the list with a loop such as

```
LinkedList<Cell> aList;
Cell *p = aList.First();

while (p) {
   // ...

   p = aList.Next();
}
```

Hint: You may want to add some private variables which keep a current pointer and/or index to the next list item.

Summary

We showed how C++ templates can be used to add additional properties to a structure or class. This technique was used to demonstrate how to set up a generic linked list class. A complete listing of a reusable linked list template class was presented and discussed.

CHAPTER 28

SIMPLEX OPTIMIZATION OF VARIABLES

I may be said to have been bisected. I am divisible into three. Through a calamity I am divisible into three.
The Gondoliers

In both instrumental and numerical aspects of scientific work, it is often desirable to have a general method for computing the best response when a number of variables must be adjusted. This can happen in adjusting a number of interacting parameters on an instrument such as the magnetic field shims of a nuclear magnetic resonance (NMR) spectrometer. It can also happen when you need to fit an equation to an arbitrary set of data and determine the coefficients of that equation that produce the best fit.

In the first case, you would simply adjust one or more of the knobs in some systematic manner and take a new reading, striving to maximize the lock signal. In the second case, you adjust the coefficients in a systematic manner, striving to minimize the distance between the computed curve and the tabulated data points.

In both cases the "systematic manner" could be the *simplex optimization* method. Rather than utilizing random or linear adjustments to the parameters, the simplex method determines each new set of parameters by looking at the quality of the last three measurements and computing how to obtain the next set. This approach was originally described by Spendley, Hart, and Himsworth,[1] and was later applied to chemical parameters by Long.[2] Reviews of the simplex procedure have been given by Deming and Morgan[3] and by Shavers, Parsons, and Deming.[4]

Since you could be trying to maximize a signal or minimize an error, we need to agree which is a "best" response in the following discussion. Since we will be illustrating the simplex procedure for fitting a function to a set of data points, we will define a best response as one with the smallest possible value. We will reflect this in our C++ examples as well.

The Simplex Method

If we wish to minimize a function of N variables, our simplex is merely a figure having $N + 1$ vertices in N dimensions. To illustrate this, we will consider the case of minimizing a function of two variables. The simplex will then have three vertices and lie in two-dimensional space.

We start the simplex procedure with a guess for each parameter and an estimated *delta* to change each of these parameters to determine two other data points. We then compute the values of the function for each of these parameter sets and rank these responses as best, next, and worst. Then, to determine which direction to vary the parameters to obtain the next measurement, we vary the parameters so that the new measurement will be as far as possible from the worst response just observed. Then these last three points are ranked and a new data point computed by reflecting away from the new worst data point. This process continues until the response cannot be improved further.

This process is somewhat difficult to grasp in the abstract but very simple to see graphically. Let us consider a simple two-parameter three-vertex simplex, which we can represent on the page in two dimensions. We start by obtaining three initial values of our function's response with the first guessed set of parameters and two more sets derived from them using the initial guessed values of delta. The response, in this case, is just the *chi-square* value of the difference between the calculated and observed data points for all the tabulated data points we are attempting to fit to the function. We obtain our first three responses and label them as B, N, and W, for best, next, and worst:

The simplex procedure then calculates the new point to measure, P, by reflecting away from the worst response, W, by simple geometry. This calculation is obvious in two dimensions, but it can be extended to any number of dimensions.

First, the average coordinates of all the data points except the worst one, P_w, are calculated. These are referred to as the coordinates of the *centroid*. This is given by

$$C = (1/n)(P_1 + P_2 + \cdots + P_{w-1} + P_{w+1} + \cdots + P_n + P_{n+1})$$

where C is a point having coordinates in all N dimensions which are the average coordinates of all but the worst point. Then the coordinates of the new data point are calculated by reflecting away from the worst point around the centroid point:

$$P_{new} = C + (C - W)$$

In the diagram below, the centroid C is shown midway between B and N, and the new data point P is shown at a distance WC on the other side of the simplex from the worst data point:

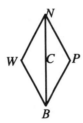

We then move on to the next simplex by evaluating the order of best, next, and worst in this second simplex, eliminating the worst point and reflecting about a new centroid, resulting in

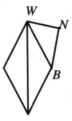

In the case where the response at the new point is the worst point of the new simplex, we would reflect right back to the old worst point of the old simplex. To circumvent the simplex being stranded in this way, we add one additional rule: if the newest point is the worst, we eliminate the next worst point N instead of the worst point and reflect across the centroid consisting of the points B and W to form the next simplex.

Summary of the Basic Simplex Procedure

1. Measure $N + 1$ data points and determine the best, next best, and worst.

2. A new simplex is created by discarding the point of the current simplex with the worst response and reflecting across the centroid of the remaining points.

3. If the reflected point has the worst response of the new simplex, form a new simplex by discarding the next worst point instead.

4. If the new vertex lies outside reasonable bounds for any parameters you are varying, return a highly undesirable response.

Disadvantages of the Basic Simplex Procedure

The basic simplex procedure can never achieve a finer measurement between points than was specified in the original distances between the first points. Consequently, you must either specify a very fine granularity, which could lead to a large number of iterations, or you must continually reinvoke the simplex procedure with finer steps to obtain the best convergence.

In addition, in cases of more than two dimensions, the simplex will not necessarily home in on the top of the desired response but will circle it rather inefficiently. This makes it difficult to determine whether to discontinue iteration or reduce the distance between points. For these reasons, a number of methods for circumventing these problems have been proposed.

The Modified Simplex Procedure

The modified simplex procedure is one of the simplest methods for avoiding the disadvantages discussed above. It has been discussed by Nelder and Mead[5] and in the reviews by Deming[3,4] and co-workers. In this procedure, the distance between points can be expanded or contracted, depending on the relationship between the points in each simplex.

1. If the new point is the best one yet obtained, expand the simplex in that direction by doubling the reflection distance cp to $2cp$. If the newer point is better, use it; but if it is worse, keep the original new point.

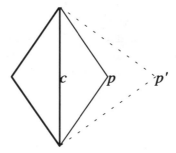

2. If the new point is worse than the next best and better than the worst, shorten the reflection axis by one-half. Use the value p' only if it is better.

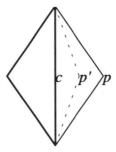

3. If the new point is worse than W, measure the response halfway between W and C and use it if it is better.

4. If none of the above are true, keep p as the new point.

In summary, the modified simplex procedure provides for expansion and contraction of the simplex where the factor F is determined by evaluating the new point p with respect to B, N, and W.

	F
$P > B$	2.0
$N < P < B$	1.0
$W < P < N$	0.5
$P < W$	-0.5

The Function to Execute

In order for a simplex program to iterate, you must provide a function which evaluates an equation for each set of parameters which the simplex procedure generates. In other languages, this function must either be inserted in or linked with the simplex code. C programmers can also pass a pointer to the function into the simplex iteration procedure.

C++ provides a much cleaner method for making a new function part of the simplex routine: *derived classes*. Suppose that we define a base Simplex class as follows:

```
class Simplex {
public:
    Simplex(unsigned int nvars = 1);     //constructor
    virtual ~Simplex();                  //destructor
    long Initialize(const double *in);   //initialize simplex
    long Optimize(double *out, double&
                    outresp);            //optimization

    virtual double GetFit(double *coef) = 0; //pure virtual
```

This partial definition contains the major features: the constructor and destructor, initialization and optimization functions, and a pure virtual function called **GetFit**. As we have noted earlier, you must define such pure virtual functions in a derived class in order to use these classes. This **GetFit** function returns the chi-square fit of the function to the user's data using the supplied coefficients.

The Query and Set Functions

The base Simplex class will also need to have member functions to examine and set these private variables:

```
// query and set functions for private variables
    unsigned long Iterations()          //Get # iterations
    void Iterations(unsigned long niter) //set them
    unsigned long Restarts()            //get # of restarts
    void Restarts(unsigned long nstarts) //set restarts

    double Tolerance()                  //Get tolerance
    void Tolerance(double tol);         //set tolerance

    double StepFactor()
    void StepFactor(double sfactor)

    unsigned int NumVariables()  //get dimensions

    virtual long Error()         // get error value
```

In the actual **Simplex** class, we can make many of these functions **inline** functions to improve the efficiency of the code.

Private Simplex Variables

In the private section, we will put the basic values we need to manipulate the simplex:

```
private:

    unsigned long NumIterations;        // number of iterations
    unsigned long NumResets;            // number of resets

    double smpTolerance;            // tolerance for end test
    double smpStepFactor;           // simplex step multiplier

    unsigned int NumDimensions;   // number of dims(variables)

    double *CurSolution;            // array of solution values
    double *Centroid;           // centroid (w/o worst vertex)
    double *test1;              // temporary reflected vertices
    double *test2;
    double **SmplxVert;         // current vertices of simplex
    double *Response;           // responses from simplex points
    double *StepSize;           // step sizes for each variable

    int isInitialized;          //Boolean set when simplex initld
    long smpError;                      // error value
```

Private Member Functions

The Simplex class also contains the functions needed to compute the simplex iterations. These are

```
    void AllocateArrays();          //allocate memory for arrays
    double GetRandomValue();     //get random numbers (-1 to 1)
    // routine to find index of vertices
    // for best, worst and next worst values
    void FindIndex(unsigned int& worst, unsigned int& next,
                unsigned int& best);
    void Reset();
    void CalcCentroid(unsigned int index);
    void CalcReflection(double *out, unsigned int index,
                    double coef);

    // routines to replace a simple vertex with a new one
    // and calculate the goodness of fit
    void Replace(unsigned int index, double *v, double resp);
    double CalcGoodfit();

    // private copy constructor and operator=
    Simplex(const Simplex&);
    Simplex& operator=(const Simplex&);
```

Fitting an Exponential Function Using the Simplex

To fit a set of data to an equation using the simplex method, we first derive a class from the base Simplex class which contains this function and a measurement of the fit of the function to the data:

```
class ExpCurv : public Simplex {

public:
    ExpCurv(unsigned int nvars);            //constructor
```

```
    void SetData(double *, long );        //put in data
    double Function(double *coef, long i); //user function
    virtual double GetFit(double *coef);
private:
    double *data;       //array of data to fit
    long datacount;    //number of data points
};
```

In this derived class, we will fit data to the function

$$y_i = a_1 + a_2 \exp(a_3 x_i)$$

This simple function is

```
double ExpCurv::Function(double *coef, long i)
{
return ( coef[0] + coef[1] * exp(coef[2]* (i+1)));
}
```

where **coef** points to an array of three coefficients and **i** is the x-index of the data.

The Matrix of Coefficients

We generate the vertices of the simplex in a two-dimensional array *a* where each column represents another measurement and each row one of the parameters. To begin, we put the initial guesses in column 1, and then using the initial increments and a random number generator, we generate the next *n* columns of parameters, so that there are *n*+1 total columns.

Our random number generator is based on the C library **srand** function, which returns a random number in the range $0 < n < 1.0$. In order to double the range to $-1.0 < n < 1.0$, we get a second random number and negate the first obtained value if it lies in the lower half of the random number range:

```
// GetRandomValue - returns a random number between -1 and 1
double Simplex::GetRandomValue()
{
    double value = (double)rand()/(double)RAND_MAX;
    if (rand() < RAND_MAX/2)
        value = -value;       //negate these randomly

    return(value);
}
```

Using this method, we start with initial guesses of 1.0, 1.0, and 1.0 and increments of 0.1, 0.1, and 0.1 and generate an initial table of coefficients of the form

1.0	0.713	0.288	0.235

1.0	1.66	1.17	1.46
1.0	1.29	0.953	0.863

The program proceeds by calculating the value of y_i for each x_i and determining the sum of the squares of the differences between the calculated y_i and the originally tabulated y_i. This sum of *chi-squared* values is the response or value for that set of coefficients. This is done in the **GetFit** routine shown below:

```
double ExpCurv::GetFit(double *coef)
  {
 // calculate estimated curve and compare with original data
    double tmp, estimate, diff, fit = 0.0;

    for (unsigned long i = 0L; i < datacount; i++)
      {
      estimate = Function(coef, i);
      diff = data[i] - estimate;
      fit += (diff*diff); //sum of squares of differences
      }

    return( sqrt( fit/(double)(datacount - 3L) ) );
}
```

For example, the responses calculated for the initial coefficients are

	Initial trial values				reflect	expand
	1.0	0.713	0.288	0.235	0.302	0.097
	1.0	1.66	1.17	1.46	.761	0.310
	1.0	1.29	0.953	0.863	0.581	0.225
response	142	24,544	1,155	707	29.73	13.24

The simplex routine recognizes that column 0 has the best response, column 3 the next best, and column 1 the worst. It determines the centroid, eliminating column 1's coordinates, and computes the next trial simplex vertex by reflection. It finds that this is a better response (smaller) and doubles the reflection distance to determine the expanded coefficients response, as described in the modified simplex rule 2. This last response is the most improved and this last column is then used to replace column 1. This process continues until the difference between responses is less than the specified tolerance or the total number of iterations has been exceeded.

Initializing the Simplex Object

In order to use our simplex object, we must initialize it. This takes place in two steps: the constructor and an initialization routine that allocates memory for the arrays of trial coefficients. We start by initializing our derived class. The **ExpFunc** class constructor is empty: we have no additional internal variables to initialize:

```
ExpCurv::ExpCurv(unsigned int nvars) : Simplex(nvars)

{
}
```

However, this constructor also calls the base class **Simplex** constructor which sets some standard iteration parameters, initializes the random number generator using the function **srand,** and allocates memory for the matrix of trial coefficients:

```
// Simplex - constructor
Simplex::Simplex(unsigned int nvars)
{
   // init private variables
   NumIterations = 500L;
   NumResets = 5L;
   smpTolerance = 1.0e-7;
   smpStepFactor = 0.7;
   NumDimensions = nvars;
   CurSolution = 0;        //set all pointers to 0
   Centroid = 0;
   test1 = 0;              //trial reflection array
   test2 = 0;              /trial expansion/contraction array
   SmplxVert = 0;
   Response = 0;
   StepSize = 0;
   isInitialized = FALSE;       //set as not yet initialized
   smpError = Simplex_NO_ERROR;

   // initialize random number generator
   srand( (unsigned int)time(0) );

   // allocate memory for arrays (sets error variable)
   AllocateArrays();
}
```

Allocating memory for the arrays is accomplished in the following private member function:

```
//Initializes memory for the internal working arrays
void Simplex::AllocateArrays()
{
   CurSolution = new double[NumDimensions];
   Centroid = new double[NumDimensions];
   test1 = new double[NumDimensions];
   test2 = new double[NumDimensions];
   Response = new double[NumDimensions + 1];
```

```
      StepSize = new double[NumDimensions];

      if (!CurSolution || !Centroid || !test1 || !test2 ||
          !Response || !StepSize) {
        smpError = Simplex_MEMORY_ALLOCATION;
        return;
      }
// allocate SmplxVert as a multidimensional array
// with N+1 rows and N cols by first allocating a linear
// array of doubles for the entire matrix
      unsigned int size = (NumDimensions + 1)*NumDimensions;
      double *p = new double[size];
      if (!p) {
        smpError = Simplex_MEMORY_ALLOCATION;
        return;
      }

      // now allocate space for the N+1 pointers (to the rows)
      SmplxVert = new double *[NumDimensions + 1];
      if (!SmplxVert) {
        smpError = Simplex_MEMORY_ALLOCATION;
        return;
      }

      SmplxVert[0] = p;     // first row points to linear array
// to allow [][] addressing of SmplxVert, set up pointers
// so start of each row points to
// a column of NumDimensions size
      for (unsigned int i = 1; i < (NumDimensions + 1); i++)
        SmplxVert[i] = SmplxVert[i - 1]
                            + NumDimensions * sizeof(double);
}
```

Setting the Initial Guessed Values

As part of our constructor, we indicated the number of coefficients we plan to vary. We will now use the initialization routine to pass in these initial guesses and call the random number generator to fill the remaining columns of the array with initial estimated values:

```
// Initialize - sets up to run the Optimization
long Simplex::Initialize(const double *guess)
{
    // check input guess array
    if (!guess)
        return Simplex_ILLEGAL_ARGUMENT;

    // put initial guess into the current solution array
    unsigned int i, j;

    for (i = 0; i < NumDimensions; i++)
        CurSolution[i] = guess[i];

    // set up step sizes to be factor of the initial values,
```

```
    // first simplex vertex is the current solution
    for (i = 0; i < NumDimensions; i++) {
        StepSize[i] = CurSolution[i]*smpStepFactor;
        SmplxVert[0][i] = CurSolution[i];
    }

    // randomize the remaining vertices of initial simplex
    for (i = 1; i < (NumDimensions + 1); i++)
        for (j = 0; j < NumDimensions; j++)
            SmplxVert[i][j] = SmplxVert[i-1][j] +
                                GetRandomValue()*StepSize[j];

    // compute fit for each of initial guesses
    for (i = 0; i < (NumDimensions + 1); i++)
        Response[i] = GetFit(SmplxVert[i]);
    // set simplex object state to initialized and return
    isInitialized = TRUE;
    return Simplex_NO_ERROR;
}
```

The Simplex Optimization Routine

Now that we have described the initialization procedure and the general algorithm, the actual optimization is quite straightforward:

```
// Optimize - carries out the simplex algorithm
long Simplex::Optimize(double *out, double& outresp)
{
    // check input arguments
    if (!out)
        return Simplex_ILLEGAL_ARGUMENT;

    // make sure object is initialized
    if (!isInitialized)
        return Simplex_NOT_INITIALIZED;

    // set up variables for carrying out the algorithm
    unsigned int i, worst, best, next;
    unsigned long num_iter = 0, num_resets = 0;
    double resp1, resp2;

    // start loop to do the simplex optimization
    int done = FALSE;

    while (!done) {
    // find the worst vertex and compute centroid of
    // remaining simplex, discarding the worst vertex
        FindIndex(worst, next, best);
        CalcCentroid(worst);        //eliminating worst

        // reflect the worst point through the centroid
        CalcReflection(test1, worst, 1.0);
        resp1 = GetFit(test1);

        // test the reflection against the best vertex
        // expand it if the reflection is better
        // if not, then keep the reflection
```

```
if (resp1 <= Response[best]) {
 // try expanding
 CalcReflection(test2, worst, 2.0);
 resp2 = GetFit(test2);
 if (resp2 <= resp1)
    Replace(worst, test2, resp2);     // keep expansion
 else
    Replace(worst, test1, resp1);     // keep reflectn
} else if (resp1 < Response[next]) {
 // new response is between the best and next worst
 Replace(worst, test1, resp1);        // keep reflectn
} else {
 // try contractions
 if (resp1 >= Response[worst])
    CalcReflection(test2, worst, -0.5);
 else
    CalcReflection(test2, worst, 0.5);

 resp2 = GetFit(test2);

 // test contracted response against worst response
 if (resp2 > Response[worst]) {
    // new contracted response is worse,
    // so decrease step size and re-start
    num_iter = 0;
    num_resets += 1;

    for (i = 0; i < NumDimensions; i++)
       StepSize[i] *= smpStepFactor;

    Reset();
    }
    Replace(worst, test2, resp2);      // keep contractn
}

// test to determine when to stop
// first check the number of iterations
num_iter += 1;     // increment iteration counter

if (num_iter >= NumIterations) {
    // restart w/ smaller steps
    num_iter = 0;
    num_resets += 1;

    for (i = 0; i < NumDimensions; i++)
       StepSize[i] *= smpStepFactor;
 Reset();
}

// limit the number of restarts allowed
if (num_resets == NumResets)
      done = TRUE;

// # of iterations and restarts have been checked
// compare relative standard deviation of vertex
// responses against a defined tolerance limit
resp1 = CalcGoodfit();

if (resp1 <= smpTolerance)
```

```
            done = TRUE;

        // if we are done, copy the best solution to the
        // CurSolution array
        // and to the output array of the calling routine
        if (done) {
            FindIndex(worst, next, best);

         for (i = 0; i < NumDimensions; i++) {
             CurSolution[i] = SmplxVert[best][i];
             out[i] = CurSolution[i];
         }

            resp1 = GetFit(CurSolution);
            outresp = resp1;
        }
    }
    return Simplex_NO_ERROR;
}
//-------------------------------------------------------------
// FindIndex - find index of vertices
// for best, worst and next worst values

void Simplex::FindIndex(unsigned int& worst,
                        unsigned int& next,
                        unsigned int& best)
{
    // initialize the return values
    worst = 0;
    best = 0;

    // find the best and worst
    unsigned int i;

    for (i = 1; i < (NumDimensions + 1); i++) {
        if (Response[i] > Response[worst])
            worst = i;
        if (Response[i] < Response[best])
            best = i;
    }

    // find the next worst index
    if (worst == 0)
        next = 1;
    else
        next = 0;

    for (i = 0; i < (NumDimensions + 1); i++) {
        if ((i != worst) && (Response[i] > Response[next]))
            next = i;
    }
}
//-------------------------------------------------------------
// Reset the simplex optimization with new step sizes

void Simplex::Reset()
{
    unsigned int worst, next, best;
```

```
    // find the current best vertex
    FindIndex(worst, next, best);

    // put best data into CurSolution array,
    // and set the first vertex
    // to the current best
    unsigned int i, j;

    for (i = 0; i < NumDimensions; i++) {
        CurSolution[i] = SmplxVert[best][i];
        SmplxVert[0][i] = CurSolution[i];
    }

    // set up remaining vertices of initial simplex
    // using the new step size
    for (i = 1; i < (NumDimensions + 1); i++)
        for (j = 0; j < NumDimensions; j++)
            SmplxVert[i][j] = SmplxVert[i-1][j] +
                             GetRandomValue()*StepSize[j];

    // initialize responses for each vector
    for (i = 0; i < (NumDimensions + 1); i++)
        Response[i] = GetFit(SmplxVert[i]);
}
//-----------------------------------------------------------
// CalcCentroid - calculate the centroid of the simplex,
// ignoring the vertex specified by index

void Simplex::CalcCentroid(unsigned int index)
{
    // calculate the centroid values
    unsigned int i, j;

    for (i = 0; i < NumDimensions; i++) {
        Centroid[i] = 0.0;        // set each variable value to 0

        // add each vertex, skipping the one given by index
        for (j = 0; j < (NumDimensions + 1); j++) {
            if (j != index)
                Centroid[i] += SmplxVert[j][i];
        }
    }

    // now divide by the number of vertices added
    for (i = 0; i < NumDimensions; i++)
        Centroid[i] /= (double)NumDimensions;
}
//-----------------------------------------------------------
// CalcReflection - calculate the reflection of the vertex
// given by index through the remaining vertices using the
// input reflection coefficient

void Simplex::CalcReflection(double *out,
                             unsigned int index, double coef)
{
    for (unsigned int i = 0; i < NumDimensions; i++)
        out[i] = Centroid[i] + coef*(Centroid[i] -
                                    SmplxVert[index][i]);
}
```

```
//------------------------------------------------------------
// Replace - replace a simplex vertex

void Simplex::Replace(unsigned int index, double *v,
                      double resp)
{
   for (unsigned int i = 0; i < NumDimensions; i++)
      SmplxVert[index][i] = v[i];

   Response[index] = resp;
   cout << "replacing " << index <<"new resp="<<resp<< " ";
   cin >> i;
}
//------------------------------------------------------------
// CalcGoodfit - calculate goodness of fit

double Simplex::CalcGoodfit() .
{
   unsigned int i;
   double avg, sd, tmp;

   // average the response values (in units of y)
   avg = 0.0;

   for (i = 0; i < (NumDimensions + 1); i++) {
      avg += Response[i];
   }
   avg /= (double)(NumDimensions + 1);

   // now compute standard deviation of responses
   // (this allows main simplex routine to compare
   // how close all simplex vertices are
   // against the tolerance)
   sd = 0.0;

   for (i = 0; i < (NumDimensions + 1); i++) {
      tmp = Response[i] - avg;
      sd += tmp*tmp;
   }
   sd /= (double)NumDimensions;

   return( sqrt(sd)/avg );
}
```

Passing Data into Our Derived Class

We have carefully avoided any reference to the type of data or where they are stored within the base **Simplex** class. We did define two private variables for this purpose in our derived class:

```
private:
   double *data;      //array of data to fit
   long datacount;    //number of data points
```

We initialize these with the **SetData** member function which simply copies the data pointer and counter into the object:

```
void ExpCurv::SetData(double *d, long npnts)
{
 data = d;
 datacount = npnts;
}
```

The Calling Routine

Our calling routine declares some test data and trial coefficients. It declares **exfunc** as an object of type **ExpCurv**, our derived **Simplex** class and inidcates that three coefficients will be used. Then, it initializes an array of three guesses to {1.0, 1.0, 1.0}, copies the data into the object, and calls the initialization routine:

```
void main()
{
   double final_coefs[3], resp;
   int err= 0;
   double tdata[] ={2.80, 3.74, 5.01, 6.74,      // test data
                 9.06, 12.20, 16.43, 22.14};
   double coefs[] = { 1.0, 1.0, 1.0};   //initial coefs
   ExpCurv exfunc(3);           // 3 coefficients to determine
   exfunc.SetData(tdata, npts);  //set the data array
   err = exfunc.Initialize(coefs);   //initialize Simplex
   err = exfunc.Optimize(final_coefs, resp);  //optimization

   // print the output results
   cout << "resp = " << resp << endl;

   cout << "coefs:" << endl
      << "a0 = " << final_coefs[0] << endl
      << "a1 = " << final_coefs[1] << endl
      << "a2 = " << final_coefs[2] << endl;
//print out fitted data points for comparison
   for (int i=0; i<8; i++)
      {
      cout << exfunc.Function(final_coefs, i) <<endl;
      }
   return 0;
}
```

Results of Simplex Computation

For the input data we provided in our calling program

1	2.80	5	9.06
2	3.74	6	12.20
3	5.01	7	16.43
4	6.74	8	22.14

the simplex routine starts with the guesses

1	1	0.1
2	1	0.1
3	1	0.1

For the equation

$$y_i = a_1 + a_2 \exp(a_3 x_i)$$

the simplex routine results in the coefficients

1	0.1
2	2.0
3	0.3

showing the curve fit to the data points in the diagram:

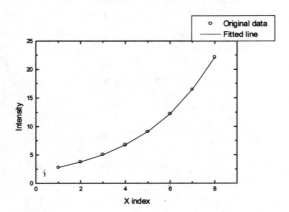

References

1. W. Spendley, G. R. Hart, and F. R. Himsworth, *Technometrics,* **4**, 441 (1962).
2. D. E. Long, *Anal. Chim. Acta,* **46**, 193 (1969).
3. S. N. Deming and S. L. Morgan, *Anal. Chem.,* **45**, 278A (1973).
4. C. L. Shavers, M. L. Parsons, and S. N. Deming, *J. Chem. Educ.,* **56**, 307 (1979).
5. J. A. Nelder and R. Mead, *Comput. J.,* **7**, 308 (1965).

CHAPTER 29

IMPLEMENTING NEURAL NETWORKS

I am but a living ganglion of irreconcilable antagonisms. I hope I make myself clear, my lady?"
"His simple eloquence goes to my heart."
HMS Pinafore

Neural networks are computerized models designed to mimic the neuronal connections of an organic brain. These models provide a framework for research in artificial intelligence and studies in the theory of learning. They are also useful in more immediate, practical ways to solve nonlinear optimization problems, learn associations, and make predictions. Neural networks have grown in popularity in the last few years, although the fundamental research in connectionist systems began over 40 years ago.[1,2]

Many problems involving pattern recognition or discriminant analysis have benefitted from the application of neural nets. Neural network models have been used in speech recognition and generation, optical character recognition, stock market prediction, and even reviews of loan applications.

This chapter presents a basic discussion of how to implement neural networks in C++.[3,4] We will show how C++ can be used to directly implement a theoretical model using the objects describing the model. You should note that direct computerization of a model is not always ideal in terms of performance. Thus, the code we present here is quite usable and extensible for your own purposes, but it is not the most efficient way to implement neural network learning algorithms. Nevertheless, it usually pays to write code in the natural "language" of the problem statement. The gain of understanding then helps if performance issues force you to rewrite the code to optimize its speed.

The Neural Net Model

The basic unit in a neural net model is the neuron, or *node*. The node is represented in Figure 1. A node can accept from one to many different inputs, and

213

each input connection has a weight associated with it. The node has a single output, which typically connects to another node.

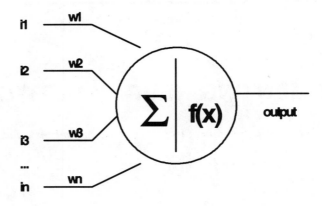

Figure 1. A schematic representation of a neuron, or node.

Nodes act in two stages: First, each input to the node is multiplied with the weight associated with its connection. The node then sums all these weighted contributions from the inputs into a single number. Second, the node applies a nonlinear transfer function, which computes its output value based on this sum. The typical transfer function used in most implementations is given by Equation 1 and plotted in Figure 2:

$$f(x) = 1/[1 + \exp(-x)] \tag{1}$$

Neural networks contain three or more *layers* of these nodes, where each layer is a linear array containing any number of nodes. The first layer is called the *input layer*, which serves as the input for a number of measurements or pattern elements used in solving a problem or doing a recognition task. The last layer is the *output layer*, which provides values or a recognized pattern associated with the inputs. The middle layer (or layers) is called the *hidden layer*, which acts in a nonlinear fashion to model the associations between the input and output patterns learned by the network.

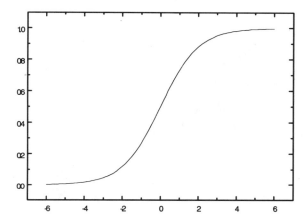

Figure 2. The nonlinear transfer function given by Equation 1.

Figure 3 shows a simple, three-layer network having two input nodes, two hidden nodes, and one output node. Each hidden node is connected to all of the input nodes, and each output node is connected to all of the hidden nodes, where each connection has an associated weight. Neural networks learn to model a problem or set of associations through the weights associated with each node's input connection. You train the network by sequentially presenting a set of training patterns to the input layer and calculating the net's response by propagating the input values through the node connections to the output layer. The values from the output layer are then compared to the desired output response for that training pattern, and the difference is used to adjust the weights in order to minimize the difference (or error).

A neural network's configuration and values of node weights determine each network's response to a particular input pattern. Networks also differ in the algorithm used to adjust the weights during training. Many algorithms have been proposed. We will show an implementation of the most popular one, the backpropagation algorithm.

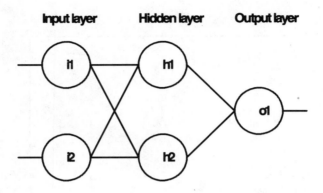

Figure 3. A three layer neural network

A C++ Implementation

The neural network model can be implemented directly in C++ using one class to describe the nodes and an abstract base class to describe a general, three-layer network. The abstract base class does all of the initialization for the array of nodes in each layer and provides methods for training and evaluation of the network. Derived classes of the abstract network class can then implement whatever learning model is desired. Our derived class will implement backpropagation.

The Node Class

We first write a class to describe an individual neuron, or node. We start by defining an enumerated type to denote whether a particular node is an input, hidden, or output layer node:

```
enum NodeType
{
    UndefinedNode, InputNode, HiddenNode, OutputNode
};
```

Here is the actual declaration for the **Node** class, which is placed along with the **NodeType** declaration above into *Node.h*:

```
class Node
{

public:
```

```
    // constructor and destructor
    Node();
    virtual ~Node();

    // initialization method
    long Initialize(NodeType type, long index,
                    long inputs);

    // compute output value or get current output value
    double Output(const double *activation);
    inline double Output() const { return myOutput; }

    // methods to access node parameters
    inline NodeType Type() const { return myType; }
    inline long Index() const { return myIndex; }
    inline long NumInputs() const { return myNumInputs; }

    // methods to get or change a weight value
    double Weight(long index) const;
    void Weight(long index, double value);

    // methods to get or modify a previous weight change
    double Delta(long index) const;
    void Delta(long index, double value);
protected:

    NodeType myType;        // node type
    long myIndex;           // node index
    long myNumInputs;       // number of inputs

    double *myWeights;      // weight for each input
    double *myDeltas;       // previous weight change

    double myOutput;        // value output by node

    // method to compute the sigmoid transfer function
    static double TransferFunction(double input);

};
```

The constructor and destructor code is straightforward, initializing and cleaning up all of the protected variables:

```
Node::Node()
{
    // init instance variables
    myType = UndefinedNode;
    myIndex = -1L;
    myNumInputs = 0L;
    myWeights = 0;
    myDeltas = 0;
    myOutput = 0.0;
}

Node::~Node()
```

```
{
    delete myWeights;    // delete arrays of weights
    delete myDeltas;     // and weight changes
}
```

The **Initialize()** method actually sets up the node by specifying its type, index number (position in the array of nodes for a particular layer), and the number of inputs coming into the node from the previous layer:

```
long Node::Initialize(NodeType type, long index,
                       long inputs)
{
    // if this is a hidden or output node, allocate
    // weight arrays and initialize them
    if ((type == HiddenNode) || (type == OutputNode)) {
        // allocate space for the weights
        myWeights = new double[inputs];
        if (!myWeights)
            return 1;   // error!

        // allocate space for the previous weight change
        myDeltas = new double[inputs];
        if (!myDeltas)
            return 1;   // error!

        // initialize the weights and weight change to 0
        for (long i = 0L; i < inputs; i++) {
            myWeights[i] = 0.0;
            myDeltas[i] = 0.0;
        }
    }

    // and save the input parameters
    myType = type;
    myIndex = index;
    myNumInputs = inputs;

    return 0;
}
```

Two arrays are also allocated and initialized to zero. These arrays represent the weight and change in the weight for each input connection between this node and all nodes in the previous layer. If the node is in the input layer, no weights are needed, so the arrays are not allocated. Note that there are inline methods that return the node type, index, and number of input connections defined after the node has been initialized.

The next method actually carries out the computation of the node's output value, based on the *activation*, or input, values from the nodes in the previous layer. The first layer simply outputs its activation value:

```
double Node::Output(const double *activation)
{
    double sum = 0.0;
```

```
    long i;

    switch (myType) {
        case InputNode:
            // output is same as input for the first layer
            myOutput = *activation;
            break;

        case HiddenNode:
        case OutputNode:
            // sum up the product of the activation inputs
            // with the weights
            for (i = 0L; i < myNumInputs; i++)
                sum += (activation[i] * myWeights[i]);

            // and apply the sigmoid transfer function
            // (the output will range from 0 to +1)
            myOutput = TransferFunction(sum);
            break;
    }

    return myOutput;
}
```

The hidden and output layer nodes calculate the weighted sum of the contributions from all of the inputs and then apply the transfer function (Equation 1) to get the output value. The sum is checked to make sure the exponential function does not overflow, and the output range is always between 0.00001 and 0.99999:

```
double Node::TransferFunction(double input)
{
    if (input > 11.5129)
        return 0.99999;
    else if (input < -11.5129)
        return 0.00001;
    else
        return ( 1.0/(1.0 + exp(-input)) );
}
```

The only other functions we need are to get and set the individual weight and weight change values for each connection. The following methods access and modify the **myWeights** and **myDeltas** array values:

```
double Node::Weight(long index) const
{
    // get weight value at the input index
    switch (myType) {
        case InputNode:
            return 1.0;

        case HiddenNode:
        case OutputNode:
            return myWeights[index];
```

```
    }

    return 0.0;
}

void Node::Weight(long index, double value)
{
    // set weight value at the input index to value
    switch (myType) {
       case HiddenNode:
       case OutputNode:
          myWeights[index] = value;
          break;
    }
}

double Node::Delta(long index) const
{
    // get delta weight value at the input index
    switch (myType) {
       case HiddenNode:
       case OutputNode:
          return myDeltas[index];
    }

    return 0.0;
}

void Node::Delta(long index, double value)
{
    // set delta weight value at the input index to value
    switch (myType) {
       case HiddenNode:
       case OutputNode:
          myDeltas[index] = value;
          break;
    }
}
```

An Abstract Network Class

Now that we have a general **Node** class, we can implement an abstract base class called **NeuralNetwork**, which defines the network configuration and provides evaluation and training functions:

```
class NeuralNetwork
{

public:

    // constructor and destructor
    NeuralNetwork(long inputs, long hidden,
                   long outputs);
    virtual ~NeuralNetwork();

    // method to randomize the weights
```

```
    long RandomizeWeights();

    // pure virtual training method which takes an input
    // and desired output pattern, and returns the
    // training error (this method must be overridden
    // in a derived class of NeuralNetwork to define the
    // training algorithm)
    virtual long Train(const double *inPattern,
                       const double *outPattern,
                       double& trainingError) = 0;

    // evaluation method that constructs an output
    // pattern from the input pattern using the current
    // network weights
    long Evaluate(const double *inPattern,
                  double *outPattern);

    // methods to access numbers of nodes
    inline long NumInputNodes() const
        { return myNumInputs; }
    inline long NumHiddenNodes() const
        { return myNumHidden; }
    inline long NumOutputNodes() const
        { return myNumOutput; }

    // methods to access node arrays
    inline Node *InputNodes() const
        { return myInputArray; }
    inline Node *HiddenNodes() const
        { return myHiddenArray; }
    inline Node *OutputNodes() const
        { return myOutputArray; }

    // methods to get and set learning rate and momentum
    inline double LearnRate() const { return myRate; }
    inline void LearnRate(double rate) { myRate = rate; }

    inline double Momentum() const { return myFactor; }
    inline void Momentum(double m) { myFactor = m; }

protected:

    long myNumInputs;     // num nodes in each layer
    long myNumHidden;
    long myNumOutput;

    Node *myInputArray;  // node arrays for each layer
    Node *myHiddenArray;
    Node *myOutputArray;

    double myRate;        // learning rate
    double myFactor;      // previous weight change factor

    double *netResult;    // temporary work arrays
    double *outputError;
    double *hiddenError;

    // methods used to initialize the network
    long Initialize(long inputs, long hidden,
```

```
                          long outputs);
    void Cleanup();

    // class method to return a random value in the
    // range [-0.5, 0.5] (the Initialize() method seeds
    // the random number generator)
    static double Random();

private:

    double *inputResult;   // temporary work arrays
    double *hiddenResult;

};
```

The constructor takes three input variables specifying the number of nodes in each layer of the network. All of the instance variables for the object are then initialized to default values. The network initialization is completed by calling an **Initialize()** method which allocates the arrays of nodes for each layer and some additional arrays to use for work areas during the training and evaluation of the network:

```
NeuralNetwork::NeuralNetwork(long inputs, long hidden,
                             long outputs)
{
    // init instance variables
    myNumInputs = 0L;
    myNumHidden = 0L;
    myNumOutput = 0L;
    myInputArray = 0;
    myHiddenArray = 0;
    myOutputArray = 0;
    myRate = 0.5;
    myFactor = 0.5;
    netResult = 0;
    outputError = 0;
    hiddenError = 0;
    inputResult = 0;
    hiddenResult = 0;

    // initialize the network
    Initialize(inputs, hidden, outputs);
    RandomizeWeights();
}
```

Here is the listing for the initialization method. It simply allocates the arrays and calls the **Initialize()** method for each **Node**. **Cleanup()** is called if any problems are encountered:

```
long NeuralNetwork::Initialize(long inputs, long hidden,
                               long outputs)
{
    // allocate space for the node arrays
    myInputArray = new Node[inputs];
```

```
if (!myInputArray)
    return 1;       // error!

myHiddenArray = new Node[hidden];
if (!myHiddenArray) {
    Cleanup();
    return 2;       // error!
}

myOutputArray = new Node[outputs];
if (!myOutputArray) {
    Cleanup();
    return 3;       // error!
}

// initialize each node in the three layers
long index, rc;

// input layer
for (index = 0L; index < inputs; index++) {
    rc = myInputArray[index].Initialize(InputNode,
                                    index, 1L);
    if (rc != Node_NO_ERROR) {
        Cleanup();
        return 4;  // error!
    }
}

// hidden layer
for (index = 0L; index < hidden; index++) {
    rc = myHiddenArray[index].Initialize(HiddenNode,
                                    index,
                                    inputs);
    if (rc != Node_NO_ERROR) {
        Cleanup();
        return 5;  // error!
    }
}

// output layer
for (index = 0L; index < outputs; index++) {
    rc = myOutputArray[index].Initialize(OutputNode,
                                    index,
                                    hidden);
    if (rc != Node_NO_ERROR) {
        Cleanup();
        return 6;  // error!
    }
}

// initialize the temporary work arrays
netResult = new double[outputs];
if (!netResult) {
    Cleanup();
    return 7;       // error!
}

outputError = new double[outputs];
if (!outputError) {
```

```
        Cleanup();
        return 8;        // error!
    }

    hiddenError = new double[hidden];
    if (!hiddenError) {
        Cleanup();
        return 9;        // error!
    }

    inputResult = new double[inputs];
    if (!inputResult) {
        Cleanup();
        return 10;       // error!
    }

    hiddenResult = new double[hidden];
    if (!hiddenResult) {
        Cleanup();
        return 11;       // error!
    }

    // initialize the number of nodes in each layer
    myNumInputs = inputs;
    myNumHidden = hidden;
    myNumOutput = outputs;

    return 0;
}
```

Once the network is initialized, the weights associated with the connections between all of the nodes are randomized by the constructor using this function:

```
long NeuralNetwork::RandomizeWeights()
{
    // seed the random number generator using the
    // current system time
    time_t cur_time;
    time(&cur_time);
    srand( (unsigned int)cur_time );

    // randomize the weights in the hidden and output
    // layers to the range [-0.5, 0.5]
    long i, j;

    // do hidden layer weights first
    Node *p = myHiddenArray;
    long num_nodes = myNumHidden;
    long num_connections = myNumInputs;

    for (i = 0L; i < num_nodes; i++) {
        for (j = 0L; j < num_connections; j++) {
            p[i].Weight(j, Random());
            p[i].Delta(j, 0.0);
        }
    }

    // now do output layer weights
```

```
    p = myOutputArray;
    num_nodes = myNumOutput;
    num_connections = myNumHidden;

    for (i = 0L; i < num_nodes; i++) {
        for (j = 0L; j < num_connections; j++) {
            p[i].Weight(j, Random());
            p[i].Delta(j, 0.0);
        }
    }

    return 0;
}
```

The standard C library random number generator is seeded with the current system time, and random numbers representing weight values between -0.5 and 0.5 are computed with the following internal method:

```
double NeuralNetwork::Random()
{
    return( 2.0*(double)rand()/(double)RAND_MAX - 1.0 );
}
```

The destructor simply calls the **Cleanup()** method used previously in the initialization routine. This deallocates any memory previously allocated and resets the array pointers to zero:

```
NeuralNetwork::~NeuralNetwork()
{
    Cleanup();
}


void NeuralNetwork::Cleanup()
{
    // delete the arrays
    delete [] myInputArray;
    delete [] myHiddenArray;
    delete [] myOutputArray;
    delete netResult;
    delete outputError;
    delete hiddenError;
    delete inputResult;
    delete hiddenResult;

    // and re-initialize the pointers to zero
    myInputArray = 0;
    myHiddenArray = 0;
    myOutputArray = 0;
    netResult = 0;
    outputError = 0;
    hiddenError = 0;
    inputResult = 0;
    hiddenResult = 0;
}
```

The final method in the abstract base class is the evaluation function, which accepts an input pattern applied to the input layer and propagates this pattern through the three layers of the network. The resulting output pattern (using the current network weight values) is returned:

```
long NeuralNetwork::Evaluate(const double *inPattern,
                             double *outPattern)
{
    // apply input pattern to the first layer and
    // propagate it to the hidden and output layers
    long index;
    double *activation;

    // compute the output of the input layer (which will
    // be the same as the input layer)
    for (index = 0L; index < myNumInputs; index++) {
        activation = (double *)&inPattern[index];
        inputResult[index] =
            myInputArray[index].Output(activation);
    }

    // propagate the input layer outputs to the hidden
    // layer (where each node takes as input all of the
    // input layer's outputs)
    for (index = 0L; index < myNumHidden; index++)
        hiddenResult[index] =
            myHiddenArray[index].Output(inputResult);

    // propagate the hidden layer outputs to the output
    // layer (where each node takes as input all of the
    // hidden layer's outputs)
    for (index = 0L; index < myNumOutput; index++)
        outPattern[index] =
            myOutputArray[index].Output(hiddenResult);

    return 0;
}
```

There are some additional inline methods declared in **NeuralNetwork** which return the number of nodes and pointers to the node arrays for each layer. Also, inline get and set methods for a learning rate and momentum term are provided. We discuss these in the next section.

Backpropagation

There are numerous learning methods that can be applied to "train" the network. Backpropagation is a popular learning algorithm which modifies the weights according to the difference, or error, between an output pattern and the desired pattern corresponding to a particular set of inputs. During training, all of the input training patterns are applied to the input layer successively. Each input generates aan appropriate response at the output layer, which is compared to the expected output. The weight values are then adjusted according to Equation 2:

$$dW_t = -\alpha\ \partial E/\partial W + \Theta\ dW_{t-1} \qquad (2)$$

where $\partial E/\partial W$ is the derivative of the output error for the current pattern with respect to the weight values.

α is the learning rate, which determines the fraction of the error that will be used to change the weights; and Θ is a momentum term which determines how much the last weight change affects the current weight change. As noted in the previous section, these parameters are included in the **NeuralNetwork** class.

You can refer to the references and the comments in the **Train()** method below for more details on the manipulation of this equation using the chain rule to get expressions for changing the weights in each layer of the network.

To implement the backpropagation or other learning algorithms, we derive a class from the abstract base class and provide a definition for the pure virtual **Train()** method:

```cpp
class BackProp : public NeuralNetwork
{

public:

    // constructor and destructor
    BackProp(long inputs, long hidden, long outputs);
    virtual ~BackProp() {}

    // training method which takes an input and desired
    // output pattern, and returns the training error
    // (this method is overridden from the abstract base
    // class to define the training algorithm)
    virtual long Train(const double *inPattern,
                       const double *outPattern,
                       double& trainingError);

};
```

The constructor takes the number of nodes in each of the three layers as arguments, passing them to the base class. There are no variables or other initializations to perform, so the derived class needs no other constructor or destructor code:

```cpp
BackProp::BackProp(long inputs, long hidden,
                   long outputs)
    : NeuralNetwork(inputs, hidden, outputs)
{
}
```

We need only define the training method in order to have a usable network. The training function uses some of the work arrays allocated by the base class, in addition to the **Evaluate()** method:

```
long BackProp::Train(const double *inPattern,
                     const double *outPattern,
                     double& trainingError)
{
    // initialize the training error to zero
    trainingError = 0.0;

    // evaluate the network with the input pattern
    if ( Evaluate(inPattern, netResult) )
        return 1;       // error!

    // save the error for each output node in
    // outputError:   d = o(1-o)(t-o)
    // (where o is the output, t is the expected output)
    long i, j;

    for (i = 0L; i < myNumOutput; i++) {
        // sum up to get total squared error
        // of (target - actual) output
        outputError[i] = outPattern[i] - netResult[i];
        trainingError += (outputError[i]*outputError[i]);

        // and multiply the difference by the derivative
        // of the sigmoid squashing function
        // f'(x) = f(x) * [1 - f(x)]
        outputError[i] *= ( netResult[i] *
                            (1.0 - netResult[i]) );
    }
    trainingError *= 0.5;    // total error on the
                             // pattern for this run

    // compute the error for each hidden node:
    // e = h(1-h)SUM(wd)
    double sum, h;

    for (i = 0L; i < myNumHidden; i++) {
        // compute sum of delta*weight for all
        // hidden-output layer connections
        // ( this is SUM(wd) )
        sum = 0.0;
        for (j = 0L; j < myNumOutput; j++) {
            sum += ( outputError[j] *
                     myOutputArray[j].Weight(i) );
        }

        // compute delta for this node ( delta =
        // e = SUM(wd) * the current node squashing
        // function derivative h(1-h) )
        h = myHiddenArray[i].Output();
        hiddenError[i] = sum * h * (1.0 - h);
    }

    // modify the weights between the hidden and output
```

```
      // layers
      double old_weight, delta, dw, old_dw;

      for (i = 0L; i < myNumOutput; i++) {
         // get delta for each output node
         delta = outputError[i];

         // and update the weights for this node
         for (j = 0L; j < myNumHidden; j++) {
            // get the old weight value and the last
            // weight change value
            old_weight = myOutputArray[i].Weight(j);
            old_dw     = myOutputArray[i].Delta(j);

            // compute the change in weight
            // (dw = r*d*h + m*dw), where r is the
            // learning rate, m is the momentum
            h = myHiddenArray[j].Output();
            dw = (myRate * delta * h) +
                 (myFactor * old_dw);

            // and store the new weight and weight change
            // values
            myOutputArray[i].Weight(j, old_weight + dw);
            myOutputArray[i].Delta(j, dw);
         }
      }

      // now do the weights between the input and hidden
      // layers
      for (i = 0L; i < myNumHidden; i++) {
         // get delta for each hidden node
         delta = hiddenError[i];

         // and update the weights for this node
         for (j = 0L; j < myNumInputs; j++) {
            // get the old weight value and the last weight
            // change value
            old_weight = myHiddenArray[i].Weight(j);
            old_dw     = myHiddenArray[i].Delta(j);

            // compute the change in weight
            // (dw = r*d*h + m*dw)
            h = myInputArray[j].Output();
            dw = (myRate * delta * h) +
                 (myFactor * old_dw);

            // and store the new weight and weight change
            // values
            myHiddenArray[i].Weight(j, old_weight + dw);
            myHiddenArray[i].Delta(j, dw);
         }
      }

      return 0;
}
```

A training error for the input pattern is returned in the third argument to this method. The user can thus monitor the training error and iterate the training until all patterns are "learned."

An Example Application

A simple test application for a neural network is the XOR problem, where the network learns to output the XOR result of two inputs (Table 1):

i_1	i_2	o_1
0	0	0
0	1	1
1	0	1
1	1	0

Table 1. XOR output o_1 based on input pattern (i_1, i_2)

Here is a function that accepts a backpropagation network and a number of training iterations. The function trains the network using the XOR pattern and returns the total training error after the last iteration. Note that we make no attempt at optimizing the code here. This is just a simple example programmed for clarity rather than efficiency:

```
double train(BackProp& net, long num_iterations)
{
    double pattern_error, total_error;
    double inPattern[2], outPattern[1];

    // start iterations
    long cur_iteration = 0L;

    while (cur_iteration < num_iterations) {
        total_error = 0.0;

        // train 1st pattern
        inPattern[0] = 0.0;        inPattern[1] = 0.0;
        outPattern[0] = 0.0;

        net.Train(inPattern, outPattern,
                pattern_error);
        total_error += pattern_error;

        // train 2nd pattern
        inPattern[0] = 0.0;        inPattern[1] = 1.0;
```

```
        outPattern[0] = 1.0;

        net.Train(inPattern, outPattern,
                    pattern_error);
        total_error += pattern_error;

        // train 3rd pattern
        inPattern[0] = 1.0;        inPattern[1] = 0.0;
        outPattern[0] = 1.0;

        net.Train(inPattern, outPattern,
                    pattern_error);
        total_error += pattern_error;

        // train 4th pattern
        inPattern[0] = 1.0;        inPattern[1] = 1.0;
        outPattern[0] = 0.0;

        net.Train(inPattern, outPattern,
                    pattern_error);
        total_error += pattern_error;

        // increment number of iterations
        cur_iteration += 1L;
    }

    return total_error;
}
```

The next function evaluates the network for each pattern:

```
void evaluate(BackProp& net)
{
    double inPattern[2], outPattern[1];

    // evaluate 1st pattern
    inPattern[0] = 0.0;    inPattern[1] = 0.0;
    net.Evaluate(inPattern, outPattern);
    cout << "0 XOR 0 = " << outPattern[0] << endl;

    // evaluate 2nd pattern
    inPattern[0] = 0.0;    inPattern[1] = 1.0;
    net.Evaluate(inPattern, outPattern);
    cout << "0 XOR 1 = " << outPattern[0] << endl;

    // evaluate 3rd pattern
    inPattern[0] = 1.0;    inPattern[1] = 0.0;
    net.Evaluate(inPattern, outPattern);
    cout << "1 XOR 0 = " << outPattern[0] << endl;

    // evaluate 4th pattern
    inPattern[0] = 1.0;    inPattern[1] = 1.0;
    net.Evaluate(inPattern, outPattern);
    cout << "1 XOR 1 = " << outPattern[0] << endl;
}
```

And here is the main program which creates a backpropagation network and uses these two functions to train and evaluate the performance of the network:

```cpp
#include <iostream.h>
#include "BackProp.h"

int main()
{
    // set up a neural network to solve XOR problem
    // using 2 nodes in the input layer, 4 nodes in
    // the hidden layer and 1 node in the output layer
    BackProp net(2L, 4L, 1L);

    // set the learning rate and momentum
    net.LearnRate(0.9);
    net.Momentum(0.9);

    // train the network
    long num_iterations = 2000L;

    double error = train(net, num_iterations);
    cout << "Training error = " << error << endl;

    // evaluate each pattern
    cout << "Evaluations using the trained network:"
        << endl;
    evaluate(net);

    return 0;
}
```

Exercises

1. Change the C++ implementation of **Node** to an abstract base class, with derived classes for **InputNode, HiddenNode,** and **OutputNode.**

2. Define a new abstract base class called **NetworkLayer** and derived classes called **InputLayer, HiddenLayer,** and **OutputLayer.** Implement the three network layers using the appropriate derived classes of **Node** in Exercise 1. Discuss the implications of modifying the **NeuralNetwork** class to use this new set of classes.

3. Rewrite the backpropagation neural network using matrices, and benchmark your program against the object-oriented model presented in this chapter.

References

1. D. Hebb, *Organization of Behavior*, John Wiley & Sons, New York, 1949.

2. F. Rosenblatt, *The Perceptron: A Perceiving and Recognition Automaton*, Cornell Aeronautical Laboratory, Ithaca, NY, 1957.

3. D. E. Rumelhart and J. L. McClelland, *Parallel Distributed Processing*, Vols. I and II, MIT Press, Cambridge, MA, 1986.

4. A. Blum, *Neural Networks in C++*, John Wiley & Sons, New York, 1992.

CHAPTER 30

DRAWING FRACTALS

I'm very good at integral and differential calculus. I know the scientific names of beings animalculus.
The Pirates of Penzance

Programs that draw representations of fractal images are quite popular. The term *fractal* was coined by Benoit Mandelbrot at IBM's T. J. Watson Research Center. Fractals have been proposed as a general representation for shapes in nature, in addition to their esthetic appeal and mathematical significance. We won't describe fractals in detail here, but instead refer you to the extensive literature available.[1-3]

In this chapter, we will show a C++ program for drawing the *Mandelbrot set*. More computing cycles have probably been used for rendering the Mandelbrot set on computer screens than any other single graphic image. We present this discussion because the mathematics needed for drawing the Mandelbrot set are simple, and we wanted to include a C++ graphics program with wide appeal.

In addition, the implementation leads to some interesting exercises on object-oriented programming. For example, our implementation can be changed to use a complex number class and to separate the computational model from the graphics presentation. Graphics also presents a number of problems in porting programs among operating systems, all of which can be handled with object-oriented techniques.

Getting Started

We can draw a Mandelbrot set representation pixel by pixel on the computer screen. To generate each pixel, we use the following iterated equation, where z and c are both complex numbers:

$$z_{n+1} = z_n^2 + c$$

Each pixel on the screen has an x and y coordinate. If we let the x coordinate correspond to the real component of a complex number and let the y coordinate correspond to the imaginary part, then the pixel at location (x,y) defines the complex number $c = x + iy$, where i is the square root of -1.

For each pixel, or c value, we use the above equation, initially setting z_0 to zero. We iterate this equation to see how fast z approaches infinity. In practice, the iteration is done either a fixed number of times (say 512) or until the magnitude of z reaches a value of 2 or greater. A color is assigned to the pixel based on the number of iterations used, which gives an indication of how fast the point approaches infinity.

The Main Program

We start by defining a main program, **mset**:

```
#include <iostream.h>
#include <stdlib.h>
#include "mandel.h"

int main(int argc, char *argv[])
{
    // create an instance of the mandel class
    mandel aView;
    if (!aView) {
        cout << "Error initializing graphics" << endl;
        return 1;
    }

    // set the coordinate system limits for x and y
    aView.XLimits(-2.0, 1.2);
    aView.YLimits(-1.2, 1.2);

    // set the number of iterations to use in testing
    // each point, using the command line argument if
    // present
    if (argc == 2) {
        int num = atoi(argv[1]);
        aView.Iterations(num);
    }

    // put the Mandelbrot set on the screen, and wait for
    // the user to press a key - then exit
    aView.Show();
    cin.ignore();

    return 0;
}
```

Our main program first creates an instance of a class called **mandel**, which will do the actual computation and graphics work. Note that the ! operator is overloaded for this class to check for errors. We will see how this is defined in the next section.

The program then defines the range we wish to plot our Mandelbrot set over using the **XLimits()** and **YLimits()** member functions. We also specify the number of iterations to use for each pixel. Note the use of the command line to obtain the number of iterations to pass to the **mandel** class **Iterations()** method.

Next, the program simply calls the **Show()** method to draw the fractal curve and then waits for the user to press a key before exiting.

The mandel Class

We first must define the **mandel** class, which does all of the graphics initialization, pixel plotting, and computational work for the main program. We place the class declaration into *mandel.h*, so it may be included by the main program and by the *mandel.C* source file. Here is the class declaration:

```
class mandel {

public:
    // constructor and destructor
    mandel();
    virtual ~mandel();

    // methods to set parameters
    void XLimits(double min, double max);
    void YLimits(double min, double max);

    inline void Iterations(long num)
    {
        myNumIterations = num;
    }

    // method to compute and show the Mandelbrot set
    // on the screen
    void Show();

    enum state { good = 0, bad = 1 };

    // method to test the object state
    inline int operator!() const
    {
        return(myState != good);
    }

protected:
    int myColumns;          // screen resolution
    int myRows;
    int myNumColors;        // number of colors

    double minX;            // graphics coordinate limits
    double maxX;
    double minY;
    double maxY;
    long myNumIterations;   // num iterations per point
```

```
    // method to compute color for a pixel
    int Color(double cx, double cy);
private:
    state myState;    // (object state (good, bad, etc.)

};
```

This class must do both the graphics initialization work and the computations for each pixel color, so we put the graphics initialization code in the constructor and clean up in the destructor. The following constructor definition assumes that the program will be compiled for an IBM or compatible PC using Borland C++ and the Borland graphics library:

```
mandel::mandel()
{
    // init instance variables
    myColumns = 640;
    myRows = 480;
    myNumColors = 16;
    minX = -1.0;
    maxX = 1.0;
    minY = -1.0;
    maxY = 1.0;
    myNumIterations = 128;
    myState = good;

    // register the Borland VGA driver
    int rc = registerbgidriver(EGAVGA_driver);
    if (rc < 0) {
        myState = bad;
        return;
    }

    // set up the graphics mode to 640x480x16 (VGA)
    int gdriver = 9, gmode = 2;
    initgraph(&gdriver, &gmode, "");

    // check for errors
    rc = graphresult();
    if (rc != grOk)
        myState = bad;
}
```

The protected variables of the class are initialized to default values that correspond to VGA screen resolution (640 x 480) in 16-color mode. The ranges for the real and imaginary parts of *c* are also defined, along with a default number of iterations.

A private variable called **myState** is also initialized with an internal enumerated type for the class called **state**, which can take on values of **mandel::good** or **mandel::bad**. Initially, the state of the object is set to **good**. Then the Borland graphics library methods for setting up the graphics mode of the system are called. If either **registerbgidriver()** or **initgraph()** fails, the object's state is set to **bad**.

Take a look back at the main program, which uses the ! operator on the instance of **mandel** just created:

```
mandel aView;
if (!aView) {
    cout << "Error initializing graphics" << endl;
    return 1;
}
```

The **if** statement calls the ! operator for the class. This method is inline in the class declaration and returns true if the **myState** variable is **bad,** or false if the object state is **good**.

The destructor also checks the state of the object. If the state is **good,** the graphics system was initialized by the constructor, so the destructor needs to clean up by calling Borland's **closegraph()** function:

```
mandel::~mandel()
{
    if (myState == good) {
        // return system to text mode
        closegraph();
    }
}
```

The two methods which set up the x and y coordinate limits for plotting the Mandelbrot set simply set the corresponding protected variables:

```
void mandel::XLimits(double min, double max)
{
    minX = min;
    maxX = max;
}

void mandel::YLimits(double min, double max)
{
    minY = min;
    maxY = max;
}
```

The other method called by the main program sets the number of iterations to use for each pixel, and this method is defined inline in the class declaration.

Plotting the Mandelbrot Set

The last two methods we need to write actually do the computational and plotting work. The public method **Show()** is called by the main program to start the process:

```
void mandel::Show()
{
    // calculate delta values for each axis
    double deltaX = (maxX - minX)/(myColumns - 1);
    double deltaY = (maxY - minY)/(myRows - 1);

    // set up x and y values
    double x, y;

    // loop over the X values (the real part of z)
    x = minX;
    for (int col = 0; col < myColumns; col++) {
        y = minY;

        // loop over the Y values (the imaginary part of
        // z)
        for (int row = 0; row < myRows; row++) {
            // find the color to plot, which will represent
            // how fast z tends toward infinity, and plot
            // the pixel
            int color = Color(x, y);
            putpixel(col, row, color);

            y += deltaY;
        }
        x += deltaX;
    }
}
```

Show() defines **deltaX** and **deltaY** as the increment represented by each pixel, based on the screen resolution and the range of x and y our plot represents. A double loop over each row and column then calls an internal protected method called **Color()** to get the color of the pixel. Once the color is found, the Borland **putpixel()** function actually plots the pixel on the screen.

The last method is **Color()**, which actually carries out the iteration of our complex function, starting at $z_0 = 0$. At each iteration, we add the complex number c to the square of z. You can verify that the computations for the real part (x) and the imaginary part (y) inside the loop correspond to $z_n^2 + c$:

```
// Color - computes color for a pixel
int mandel::Color(double cx, double cy)
{
    // set up parameters to test z
    double x = 0, y = 0, xsquared = 0, ysquared = 0;
    int color = 1;

    // loop until the magnitude of z is greater than 2,
    // or until the number of iterations is exhausted,
    // using z0 = 0 in the equation:
    //          z(n+1) = z(n)*z(n) + c
    // where cx and cy are the real and imaginary parts
    //of c
```

```
while ((color < myNumIterations) &&
       ( (xsquared+ysquared) < 4.0 )) {
    xsquared = x*x;
    ysquared = y*y;

    y = 2*x*y + cy;
    x = xsquared - ysquared + cx;

    color += 1;
}

// limit the color value to a range of colors
return(color % myNumColors);
}
```

Figure 1 shows the result of running this program using 512 iterations for each pixel.

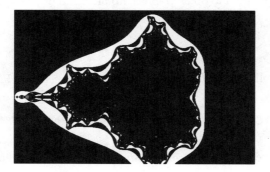

Figure 1. Output from the fractal drawing program

Exercises

1. Write a complex number class, with a complete set of overloaded operators. Use this class to write another implementation of the **mandel** class. List some trade-offs between performance and simplicity.

2. As written, the **mandel** class incorporates both graphics functions and computations. A more object-oriented approach would probably separate the computational aspects from the actual graphics. Redesign the program in a more object-oriented fashion to separate the model (or computation) from the view (or plot).

3. Our implementation was written specifically for Borland's graphics library. Extend the object-oriented model you developed in Exercise 2 to use an abstract base class that defines the graphics initialization and plotting

methods. Derive a class from this abstract base class that uses the Borland graphics functions.

4. Port your program from Exercise 3 to another operating system by deriving another class from your abstract graphics class to implement the new operating system's native graphics functions.

5. Add a user interface to the program to allow exploration of different scales of the Mandelbrot set using user-supplied X and Y plotting limits.

Summary

We presented a complete graphics program for the IBM PC using the Borland C++ graphics library for drawing the Mandelbrot set. Exercises for rewriting and extending the program to other graphics libraries and operating systems were also given.

References

1. B. Mandelbrot, *The Fractal Geometry of Nature*, W. H. Freeman and Company, New York, 1983.

2. H. O. Peitgen and D. Saupe, *The Science of Fractal Images*, Springer-Verlag, Berlin, 1988.

3. R. T. Stevens, *Fractal Programming in C*, M&T Publishing, Redwood City, CA, 1989.

A BRIEF INTRODUCTION TO THE C LANGUAGE

As he says, a British seaman is anyone's equal excepting his, and if Sir Joseph says that, is it not our duty to believe him?
HMS Pinafore

The C language was developed at Bell Laboratories for research use and is characterized by a number of features that make it ideal for scientific use. In particular, all floating point calculations are automatically carried out in double precision. Because of the early slow teletypewriter terminals, C also has a penchant for terseness that does not make it easy for the beginner to read some C code.

In the examples here, we will try to help the reader new to C overcome these problems by carefully commenting our code and trying to make it as readable as possible.

This chapter is not a complete tutorial on the C language, but only an outline of its high points. If you need to learn the entire language, there are a number of excellent texts available.

Advantages of C

Structure

One of the great advantages of the C language is that it gives the programmer the ability to write *structured* programs. In particular, you can write loops that have clear entry and exit conditions and can write functions whose arguments are always checked for correctness.

Bit Manipulations

C provides functions for setting and clearing bits and rotating them in words, which is a particularly useful concept for setting and clearing registers on interface cards in your PC.

Compactness

C is actually a fairly simple language: a number of the features that have been embedded in other computer languages are relegated to library routines in C, making the base language quite compact and easy to learn.

The C Compiler

A large number of compilers have been written for the C language that compile code for virtually any computer system you can name. The C compilers are programs that translate the source code written with the help of a text editor program into code for the specific computer on which you wish to run your program. The compilers generally produce *object modules* that typically have the .OBJ extension (on PCs) or .o extension (on Unix machines). This object module is linked with standard library routines using a linker program to produce an executable code file, having the .EXE extension on PCs or no extension under Unix.

Data Types in C

C allows you to manipulate data as various types that are handled and checked for consistency by the C compiler. The data types that C handles are

int	The integer data type. In PCs, this is generally a 16-bit integer, but this will certainly vary with the computer's architecture.
char	The basic character type. In some machines, this may be the same as an integer, and in others it may be an 8-bit byte. In all cases, the char type is automatically converted to an integer where needed during calculation without warning the user of this conversion.
long	A long integer. In PCs this is a 32-bit integer.
float	This is the shortest floating point representation in your computer. In the PC, this is a 32-bit number in IEEE standard floating point format. A floating point number allows you to represent scientific data from about

1.0E-38 to 1.0E38, where the *E* means that the number is multiplied by 10 (not *e*) raised to that power.

double The double precision floating point representation for that computer. It allows you to represent numbers to greater precision and, usually, to higher dynamic range as well. In the PC environment, double precision allows variables from -1.797E308 to -4.94E-324 and 4.94E-324 to 1.797E308.

Numbers in C

All numbers without a decimal point in C programs are treated as integers and all numbers with a decimal point are considered to be double-precision floating point. If you want to represent base-16 (hexadecimal) or base-8 (octal) numbers, you precede the number with '0x' for hexadecimal and just '0' for octal.

If you want to specify that an integral value is to be stored as a long integer, you must follow it with an "L":

```
015          /*octal 15 or 13 decimal*/
0x15         /*hex 15 or 21 decimal   */
152L         /*long integer 152       */
```

Writing a Simple C Program

For our first C program, let us write a program to add together two floating point numbers and print out the result. Initially, we won't bother to read the numbers in, but instead will simply use values stored in the program:

```
/********************ADD2***************************/
/** A C program to print out the sum of two numbers ***/
#include <stdio.    /* contains definitions of printf */
/*----------------------------------------------------*/
void main(          /* main has no return value         */
{                   /* beginning of routine             */
   double a, b, c   /* declare the variables used       */

a = 2.3             /* assign values to the variables */
b = 4.5;

c = a + b           /* add them together                */
                    /* print out the result             */
printf ("The sum is %f \n", c);

}                   /* end of the program               */
```

Observations on the ADD2 Program

There are a number of simple observations we can make about this simple program that hold for all C programs.

1. Comments begin with a /* and end with a */. Comments in this program are all less than a line long but may, in fact, be many lines long.

2. The **#include** statement describes a file that is to be read in and used as if it were part of the program at this point. The file *stdio.h* contains function definitions for standard input and output routines, which in this case include the **printf** statement used in the program. ANSI standard C requires these include files to describe the number and types of variables that may be put in any functions called by your program.

3. The main routine of any C program is always called **main()**. This is where the program starts, regardless of how many routines the program contains.

4. The actual program code begins with a left brace ({) and ends with a right brace (}).

5. Every statement ends with a semicolon (;). Complex mathematical expressions or any other kind of statement may run on for several lines if necessary. The statement only stops when the semicolon is found.

6. All variable names must be declared in advance by name and type. In this program, the three variables are all of type **double.**

7. The equals sign is used to assign values to variables. Thus
```
    a = 4.3;
```
means "put the value 4.3 in the location where the variable **a** is stored."

8. You can print out results using the **printf** statement. This statement consists of a *format string* and a list of variables.

9. The backslash character (\) in C has a special meaning. In the **printf** statement, it is used to represent the nonprinting character that causes a new line to start. This is written as "\n."

Strings and Characters in C

A single character that is used as a constant **char** is enclosed in *single quotes*:

```
    char letter;        /* "letter" is of type char */

    letter = 'a';       /* assign it the value      */
                        /* of the character a       */
```

A series of characters, however, becomes a quoted *string* and is enclosed in *double quotes*:

```
printf("hello there");
```

A string is simply an array of characters terminated with a NULL byte. It is this NULL byte that determines the length of the string.

There are a series of special nonprinting characters that are represented by preceding them with a backslash. The backslash itself is printed by preceding it with a backslash:

\n	new line character (carriage return)
\t	tab character
\b	backspace
\f	form feed
\0	null character (usually a zero byte)
\"	double quote
\'	single quote
\\	backslash

Arrays in C

In C, all arrays start at an index of 0 and have a final index 1 less than the array's dimensions. You can declare an array of values in C by simply enclosing the number of elements in the array in brackets following the variable name:

```
float freq[500];          /*array of 500 values*/
```

In this case the first element is

```
freq[0]
```

and the last element

```
freq[499]
```

Two-dimensional arrays are represented as arrays of arrays as follows:

```
float xmatrix[100][100];  /* 100 x 100 matrix */
```

Elements in these arrays are stored by rows, and the rightmost subscript varies the fastest. As we will see later, this somewhat awkward construction is seldom used because of the common use of pointers in C.

Characters and Strings in C

An individual character variable of type **char** is generally one byte long in C. A *string* of characters is simply an array of characters

```
char name[80];          /*80-character string*/
```

However, unlike some other languages, C does not allow you to operate directly on strings and assign them to variables. Thus, to copy a string into a string variable, you use the common string library function **strcpy**:

```
strcpy(name, "Anastasia");
```

Variable Names in C

Variable names in C can consist of letters, numbers, and the underscore character. They can be uppercase or lowercase or a mixture of cases. Unlike many other languages, the case of the characters is significant!

Thus the variables

```
Temperature = TEMPERATURE + temperature;
```

are all *different*! There are no real restrictions on the length of variable names, but various compilers may restrict the number of characters they actually compare to see if two names are identical.

You can use the case sensitivity and the underscore to improve the readability of variable names. Some examples include

```
SumOfPairs
sum_of_pairs
WinMessageBox
```

Arithmetic Operations

In C, you can perform the usual arithmetic operations on variables and constants using the usual operators:

+	addition
-	subtraction

*	multiplication
/	division
%	modulo (remainder after integer division)

C also has a number of bit operators for performing operations on words:

>>	shift right
<<	shift left
&	bit AND
|	bit OR
^	bit XOR
~	1s complement

Note that there is no exponentiation operator. You can call library routines for these less common functions.

The Bit Operations

You can AND, OR, or XOR together two computer words using the above operators. Remember that AND means that a bit is 1 if both of the input bits are 1s, and OR means that a bit is 1 if *either* of the input bits is a 1. The XOR operation turns on the resulting bits if the two input bits are *different*.

The #define Declaration

C allows you to define a symbolic name for any expression. At the most basic level this allows you to make use of named constants that can be changed by changing only their definition:

```
#define PI 3.1416

y = 2 * PI * r;            /*circumference*/
```

Note that the use of the symbol PI actually improves the readability of the expression and makes it clear what the constant means. By convention, C programmers usually make the names of constants all uppercase letters.

The **#define** declaration is actually a directive to a C *preprocessor* program that simply scans the code and substitutes the second expression for the first.

Thus, you are not limited to numerical values but can in fact substitute whole expressions for particular symbols.

Note that the **#define** directive does *not* end with a semicolon, since it is not a statement. If you put a semicolon on the line with a **#define** directive, it becomes part of the expression that is to be substituted.

The printf Function

In our first C program, ADD2, we introduced the **printf** function, which consists of a format string and a list of variables. This format string is quite powerful and versatile -- we will only summarize the more common features here:

```
char formatstring[nn];
printf("quotedstring", var1, var2, ...,var_n);

        /* OR */

printf( formatstring, var1, var2, ...,var_n);
```

The format string can contain
- text to be printed out
- control characters as part of the text
- format specifiers for variables

All of the format specifiers start with a % sign. The most common of these are

%f	floating point value
%d	integer value
%c	character
%s	character string

You can specify a desired field width in these specifiers by preceding the format character with a number,

```
%6d    /* 6 digit integer          */
%20s   /* 20-character string       */
```

and can add a precision field for floating point numbers,

```
%8.2f   /* width of 8, 2 decimal places */
```

There is no distinction between floating point and double-precision numbers because all such operations are carried out in double precision:

```
float a;                    /* define types */
int j;

a =  4.26;
j = 12;
printf("The %dth value is %10.4f \n",j, a);
```

will print out

```
The 12th value is      4.2600
```

The sprintf Function

The **sprintf** function performs exactly the same operations as the **printf** function, except that the characters are written into the character array (or string) you specify. The function

```
char buf[80];
float sum;

sprintf(buf, "The sum is %8.2f", sum);
```

writes the string "The sum is " followed by the current value of **sum** into the string **buf**.

Within most graphical user interfaces, we almost never use the **printf** function, but often we will write to a text buffer using **sprintf** and then call a function to display the result.

Making Decisions in C

The **if-else** statement is the most common way to make decisions in C:

```
if (KelvinTemp >= 273.16)
    printf("Water is liquid \n");
else
    printf("Water is solid \n");
```

This statement says that if the condition in the parentheses is true, execute the first statement, and if the condition is false, execute the second statement. It is also possible to write if statements without else clauses:

```
if (Denom <= 1.0e-30)
    printf("Can't divide by 0! \n");
```

There is, of course, no requirement that the statements under the if and else be indented, but it makes reading them somewhat easier.

Blocks of Statements in C

The C language is considerably more powerful than might be indicated by the above simple example. You can write entire **blocks** of statements that are to be executed when a condition is true or false. These blocks are enclosed in the same braces used to begin and end the C program:

```
r = b*b - 4.0 * a ;             /* value to take root of */
if (r >= 0                      /* if >0 calc. the roots */
    {
    x1 = (-b + sqrt(r))/(2.0 * a);
    x2 = (-b - sqrt(r))/(2.0 * a);
    printf("The roots are: %f and %f \n", x1, x2);
    }
else
                                /*or print error message */
    printf("The roots are imaginary\n");
```

Comparison Operators in C

In C, most of the symbols used to compare two numbers with each other are two characters long. A couple of them are different than in other languages, as you note from the table.

>	greater than
<	less than
>=	greater than or equal to
<=	less than or equal to
==	equal to
!=	not equal to

Note in particular that if you wish to see if two variables are *equal,* you must write *two* equals signs:

```
    if (a == b)
        printf("they are equal \n");
```

In C, nearly anything you write is a legal expression, and the expression

```
    if (a = b)                  /*mistake ! */
```

returns the value of **a** after assigning the value in **b** to it. This is the single most common programming mistake in the C language, and it is often difficult to spot because the compiler regards it as a perfectly legal statement! Note also that the "not equal" symbol is "!=" rather than the "<>" used in most other computer languages.

Combining Comparisons

If you want to perform some action based on two or more comparisons, you will need to combine their results. This is done using the logical operators for AND, OR, and NOT:

&&	AND
‖	OR
!	NOT

These represent the most commonly confused symbols in C. The *single* "&" and "|" represent bitwise operations on a number. The **double** "&&" and "‖" are operators used in combining two logical expressions:

```
if ( ( a == b ) && ( c == d))
    printf("both are equal \n");
```

Note the distinction C makes between the NOT operator and the 1's complement operator. The "!" operator negates a logical value: so a TRUE value becomes FALSE and vice versa. The "~" operator inverts all the bits in an integer: all 1s become 0s and all 0s become 1s.

You might find it easier to keep these symbols straight if you use a **#define** declaration to name them:

```
#define        OR         ||
#define        AND        &&
#define        BitAND     &
#define        BitOR      |
#define        MOD        %
#define        NOT        !
#define        OnesComp   ~
```

The switch Statement

The **switch** statement provides a succinct way of making multiple choices when a variable might have one of a number of possible values. It has the general form

```
switch (variable)
   {
```

```
case CON1:
   statements; /*execute if variable == CON1 */
   break;
case CON2:
case CON3:
   statements; /*execute if variable = CON2 or CON3*/
   break;
default:
   statements; /*execute if none of the above   */
   break;
}
```

The variable must be an integer or character variable, and the case selection values must be constants. The default case is optional, and no statement is executed if the variable does not match any constant and there is not any **default** statement.

Note carefully the **break** statement after every case. If it is not included, the statements on the lines that follow will be executed. For example, suppose we wish to convert certain characters to their Greek equivalents:

```
char c;        /* variable containing a character */

switch (c)
   {
   case 'a':
      c = 224; /* ASCII value for alpha in PC font */
      break;
   case 'b':
      c = 225; /* ASCII value for beta in PC font */
      break;
   }
```

In this case, we do nothing to **c** if there is no match, so no default statement is needed.

You can also use the **break** statement to jump out of the current block or loop, but this leads to code that can be very hard to follow, and this is not recommended.

The Ornery Ternary Operator

The statement

```
if (a > b)
   z = a;
else
   z = b;
```

can be more compactly written using the "?:" ternary operator:

```
z = (a > b) ? a : b      /* z is a if a >b, else z is b*/
```

Actually modern compilers generate the same code for either expression, and the only criterion for choice between them is readability. On this basis, we will not use the ternary operator in this text.

Increment and Decrement Operators

Because C was developed when compilers weren't as "smart" as they are today, a number of C's constructions are designed to tell the compiler the simplest way to compile the code. Many of these terse operations are surprising to scientists used to working in other languages.

You can increment or decrement any integer or long integer variable in the same expression that uses it in a calculation by either preceding or following it with "++" or "--". If the symbols precede the variable, it is incremented or decremented before it is used, and if they follow, the variable is changed after it is used:

```
i++;              /* same as i = i + 1                */
x[i++] = 12;      /* put 12 in x[i] and increment i */
y[--j] = i;       /* decrement j and put the value  */
                  /* of i in y[j]                   */
```

These auto-increment functions can be rather dangerous, since it is possible to write expressions containing several instances of a variable and become confused about when the variable is incremented.

Whenever you want to perform any of the simple arithmetic operations on a variable and put the result back into that variable, you can do that with the combination operations that simply say perform the operation on that variable:

```
j += 2;           /* j = j + 2                        */
x *= 5;           /* multiply x by 5                  */
i -= j;           /* subtract j from i                */
k /= 4;           /* divide k by 4                    */
reg >>= 2;        /* shift reg 2 places to the right */
word <<=1;        /* shift word 1 place left          */
```

Note that modern compilers would probably generate the same code from the longer expressions for the same operations, but these have a certain succinctness that makes them appealing when involved in complex expressions, as we will see in the following section on looping.

Looping Statements

For Loops

You can write loops in C using three different constructions. For loops where the lower and upper bounds are known in advance, the **for** loop is the simplest:

```
for (i = 0;  i < count; i++)
  x[i] = i;          /* put the value of i in each element*/
```

Note that since arrays always start at zero and end one before the final dimension size, we start our **for** loop at zero and loop while the index is *less than* the final count.

These for loops can contain more complex operations and are not limited to incrementing the index by 1:

```
for (i = 0; i < (count / 2); i += 2)
       x[i] *= i;
```

The **for** loop can also operate on a block of statements:

```
for (i = 0; i < count; i++)
   {
   x[i] = y[i];
   y[i] = y[i] / 3;
   }
```

In summary, the three statements in the **for** loop consist of the starting condition, the ending condition, and what to do at the end of each pass through the loop. Since the loop conditions are checked before the loop is executed, it is possible that in some cases the loop will not be executed at all.

While Loops

The **while** loop performs operations in the loop until the condition specified becomes true. As with the **for** loop, the condition is checked before the loop is executed, and the loop might not be executed at all. The while-loop has the general form

```
while (condition)
   {
   statements;
   }
```

It is generally used when a loop is to be executed an unknown number of times but will exit when some computed condition is fulfilled:

```
factorial = 1;          /*initialize factorial     */
while (num > 0)
   {
   factorial *= num;    /*multiply by current number */
   num-- ;              /*reduce num by 1           */
   }
```

You should note that a common programming error is forgetting that the variables you are testing must have initial values before you begin the **while** loop. In the fragment above, **num** must have a positive, non zero value for the loop to be executed.

The do-while Loop

The **do-while** loop looks rather like the **while** loop:

```
do
   {
   statements;
   }
while (condition);
```

It differs only in that the loop is always executed *at least once* since the test for the termination condition takes place at the end of the loop.

You should only use it when you are sure that there can never be conditions when the loop should not be executed. As you might expect, you can usually write programs to use either type of **while** loop, and the first type seems to be favored.

Pointers in C

The most unusual feature of C compared to other high-level languages is its use of *pointers*. A pointer is simply the *address* of a variable or of the beginning of an array. In C, the "&" operator means take the address of a variable, and the "*" operator means get the value pointed to by the pointer:

```
float x, y, *p; /* p is a pointer to a        */
                /* floating point number      */

p = &x;         /* get the address of x       */

y = *p;         /* y is assigned the same value as x */
                /* and pointed to by p         */
```

Pointers are very commonly used instead of array variables, since they can be incremented as you pass through a loop, without the overhead of calculating the base of an array and adding an index to it each time:

```
#define MAX 100
float x[MAX], *p;
int i;

p = x;          /* p points to beginning of array   */
for (i = 0; i < MAX; i++)
    *p++ = 0;   /* zero out the array               */
```

C automatically increments pointers by the amount suitable for the size of variable they represent: 1 byte for **char**, 2 for **integer**, 4 for **float**, and 8 for **double** on the PC, so you needn't have any knowledge of these relative sizes.

Note that this is entirely equivalent logically to

```
for (i=0; i < MAX; i++)
     x[i] = 0;
```

but may execute more rapidly, since there is no array-indexing calculation in each loop.

Pointers are also used to point to memory that is allocated and de-allocated within a module using memory management functions such as **malloc**:

```
#include <malloc.h>
int i;
float *x, *p;
                /* allocate 1000 floating pt numbers */
x = malloc(1000 * sizeof(float));
p = x;          /* use p as variable ptr             */
for (i=0; i < 1000; i++)
    *p++ = i    /* convert i to float and store      */
```

Strings as Pointers

Since strings are arrays of characters and since the name of an array is in fact a pointer to its first element, you should recognize that string variable names are in fact always pointers to the strings:

```
char string[80], *ch;

ch = string;    /* set pointer to start of string    */
```

Converting Between Data Types in C

C will automatically convert between type **char** and integers. It will make all other conversions, as well, but will warn you that it is making them. Thus, in the above example, we could have written

```
*p++ = (float)i;          /*convert integer to float*/
```

and would have avoided a warning message from the compiler. The conversion of variables from one type to another in C is called *casting* and is accomplished by preceding the variable with the new type name in parentheses.

Pointers have types associated with them as well. For example, the **malloc** function returns a pointer to variables of type **void** (a pointer to no type), and it must be cast to point to type **float**.

This casting is important, since incrementing a pointer of the wrong type may increment it by the wrong number of bytes:

```
float *x;
                      /* x is a pointer to 1000 floats */
x = (float *)malloc(4000);
```

Functions in C

While many languages provide both subroutines and functions, the C language provides only functions. A C function can have many variables and can return a single value of any simple type as an answer.

All functions are assumed to return a value of type **int** unless another type is specifically declared:

```
float xsum( float a, float b)
/* returns the sum of a and b */
{
    float sum;              /* local variable   */
 sum = a + b;
 return(sum);
}
/*----- main routine starts below---------- */
void main()
{
        float x, y, tsum;
 x = 5.0;
 y = 6.3;

 tsum = xsum(x, y);      /*call the function */
}
```

When you want to write subroutines that do not return values, you simply write functions of type **void** that return no value.

Unlike many other languages, all arguments to a function are passed *by value*. In other words, a *copy* of the variable's value is passed to the function, leaving the original intact.

This does not turn out to be much of a problem, however, because you can always pass a *pointer* to any variable to the function, and it will then have access to the original data. This is particularly useful when you want to pass a whole array to a function:

```
/* Function to sum up an array */
float arraysum(float *x, int count)
   {
   float sum;
   int i;
   sum = 0.0;                    /* initialize sum  */
   for (i=0; i<count; i++)
      sum += *x++;
   return(sum);
   }
/*------main routine starts below-------------*/
  main()
   {
   float x[100], sum;
/** code to put something in array must go here**/
   sum = arraysum(x, 100);   /* add it all together */
   }
```

Note that an array name is actually exactly the same thing as a pointer. The address of the beginning of the array **x** is the same as the value of the pointer **x**.

Static and Automatic Variables

Variables declared for use within a function usually exist only while the function is being called. Thus, if you call the function again later, a new space is created for this variable and the previous value will not be remembered. Such variables are called *automatic variables*.

Since you usually are done with such variables when you exit from a function, you usually don't care if the values are remembered. There are occasions, however, when you may call a function once to initialize some variables and again later to perform some calculations.

In this case you want these variables to be remembered. In C these are called *static variables* and are denoted by preceding the variable type with the keyword **static**:

```
void statfunc(int a, float x)
```

```
{
    double gronch;      /* automatic variable */
    static int brunch; /* static variable    */
```

Function Prototypes

When you write a function that is called from within a module or, more important, from another module, the C compiler must know the number and type of arguments and the return type of the function. You provide these by simply declaring the function at the top of each module using the same declaration as you used at the beginning of the function, except that you follow it with a *semicolon.*

If your function starts with the statement

```
void statfunc(int a, float x)
```

you would put the following statement at the top of all modules that call that function:

```
void statfunc(int a, float x);
```

Since this can lead to errors very quickly as you change functions, it is more common to put these declarations in an *include file* that you reference at the beginning of each module:

```
#include "statf.h"
```

where this file may include declarations for a number of related functions.

A large number of include files are provided with your C compiler, which are typically kept in a standard **include** subdirectory for that compiler. These include files define the variable types and return types for all of the C library routines. The C library manual for your compiler will tell you which files to include.

If you enclose the filename for the include file in *angle brackets*, C will look in the compiler's \include directory or that directory list defined by the operating system's **include** environment variable. If you enclose the filenames in quotes, C will only look for them in the current directory.

The scanf Function

Until now, we have avoided explaining how to read in data from the keyboard. This is because the **scanf** function requires the use of pointers. It has the form

```
scanf("%f %d", &x, &j);
```

where the format strings have the same meaning as they did for **printf** but the values passed to the routine are *pointers* to the actual variables. There is also an analogous routine **sscanf** that operates on a character buffer:

```
sscanf(buf, "%f %d", &x, &j); /*convert from buffer*/
```

As we noted above, strings are always pointers, so that if you are reading in data to a string, the name of the string array is *not* preceded with the "&" sysmbol:

```
char st[80];
int i;

scanf( "%d %s", &i, st);   /* read integer and string */
```

File Handling in C

The file handling calls in C are **fopen, fclose, fread, fgets, fputs, fputc,** and **fgetc**. These all utilize a pointer to a **FILE** structure:

```
#include <stdio.h>
FILE *f;
char string[80];

f = fopen("filename.ext", "r"); /*open a file -read only */
if (f != NULL)
   {
   fgets(string, 80, );   /*read a string from the file*/
   fclose(f;              /*close the file            */
   }
```

You should note that the pointer **f** will be NULL if the file can't be found, and that performing an **fclose** on a null pointer will crash your program. Further, the **fgets** function reads a string to first end-of-line or end-of-file mark and *includes* this new line character (**\n**) in the string that is read. Often you must write code to remove that character from the string.

General C Library Functions

There are a large number of functions provided with the compiler for many types of operations. These are described in the C Library Reference manuals provided with your compiler. When you call these functions, be sure to add the **#include** header files specified for that function in the reference manuals.

Structures in C

The last topic in our survey of C is the *structure*. A structure is a group of related variables of various types that are kept together. This turns out to be a very important concept in GUI programming, because descriptions of files, windows, and other internals are all kept as structures. To define a structure you simply begin by writing it out following the **struct** keyword, with all of the variables enclosed in braces:

```
struct fblock
    {
    float x, y;          /*two fp variables*/
    int i, j;            /*two integers    */
    char name[80];       /*and a string    */
    };
```

The name **fblock** is the name of this structure and can be used to represent it without listing its elements again when we define actual variables of this structure type. Note particularly that the structure definition ends, like all statements, with a semicolon. Omission of this semicolon is a common programming error that leads to untold confusion by many compilers.

Then to declare variables of this structure type, we simply write

```
struct fblock f1, f2;    /*two structure variables    */
```

Elements within a structure are accessed by adding a period to the structure variable name and following it with the name of the element:

```
f1.x = 4.32;             /*floating element           */
f1.j = 12;               /*integer element            */
strcpy(f1.name, "foo");  /*put string into structure */
```

Pointers to Structures

You can allocate space for structures dynamically in your C program using the **malloc** function. Since we don't know the size of a structure in general, we can use the C **sizeof** function to calculate it for us:

```
struct fblock *pf;       /*pointer to structure */

/*allocate space for a structure*/
pf = (struct fblock *)malloc(sizeof(struct fblock));
```

This returns a pointer to a memory space where the structure is to be located. A special character pair "->" has been defined in C to get the value of a structure element where the base name is a pointer to the structure rather than the structure itself:

```
/*allocate space for a structure*/
pf = (struct fblock *)malloc(sizeof(struct fblock));

pf->x = 4.5;                    /*assign value to element   */
strcpy(pf->name, "fred"); /*copy string into structure*/
```

The typedef Declaration

The **typedef** declaration provides a way for you to declare names for new data types. You could write

```
typedef struct fblock
    {
    float x, y;            /*two fp variables */
    int i, j;              /*two integers     */
    char name[80];         /*and a string     */
    } FBLOCK, *PFBLOCK;
```

Now you have defined the type **FBLOCK** as the type

```
struct fblock
```

and **PFBLOCK** as a pointer to that structure type. Then you can declare your variables and allocate structures more simply:

```
PFBLOCK pf;          /*pointer to structure */

/*allocate space for a structure*/
pf = (PFBLOCK)malloc(sizeof(struct fblock));
```

Comments in C

Since C can be so terse, comments are absolutely required to make C programs readable. As we noted earlier, a comment starts with "/*" and ends with "*/." You can continue a comment for several lines, but this can lead to lost beginnings and endings of comments. If a comment describing a program's purpose or function will carry on for a number of lines, it is customary to start each line with "/*" and end each line with "*/" to make the comment stand out for the reader. Contrast the two examples below:

```
/* This is a comment at the beginning of a program
This program is used to read in columns of scientific
data and display them on the screen as xy plots. Each
successive column is displayed in a distinct color. */
    or
/*---------------------------------------------------------*/
/* This is a comment at the beginning of a program       */
```

```
/* This program is used to read in columns of scientific */
/* data and display them on the screen as xy plots. Each */
/* successive column is displayed in a distinct color.   */
/*-------------------------------------------------------*/
```

Since it is often useful to be able to "comment out" single lines of code in a program under development, recent C standards have also added the double slash ("//") as the beginning of a single-line comment. Any line that starts with two slashes is treated as a comment:

```
c = a + b;      /* This line is compiled */
//c = a + b;    /* This line is skipped  */
```

Macros in C

The **#define** statement in C can also be used to make some complex expressions appear simpler to the reader. Define statements that make use of arguments are called **macros**. For example, we could define a macro to get the upper 16 bits of a 32-bit word by

```
#define UPPERWORD(a)  (((a) >> 16) & 0xffff)
```

and the **max** function is often implemented as a macro:

```
#define max(a, b) ((a) > (b) ? (a) : (b))
```

Structured Programming in C

A structured program is one that follows a few simple rules that make it easy to read and maintain. Some of these are:

1. Each function or routine must have a clearly distinguishable purpose. You should set off each function within a module with a line of asterisks or dashes and start it with a comment explaining its purpose.

2. Every routine should have only one entry and exit point. You should be able to start at the beginning of a routine and know that code will be executed starting there, and be sure that code at the end of a routine will be executed last. This precludes the use of **goto** statements that disturb linear program flow. Use **if-else** and **while** statements to control program flow.

3. A loop or block should only exit at the *bottom*. While the **goto** and **break** statements could be used to exit prematurely from a loop, it is better to use flags and **if** statements instead. The same amount of code is generated in either case and the code is easier to read.

You should align the block of code under the brace delimiters and indent the whole block. Be sure to put spaces between all variable names and their operators.

```
/*---good indentation and spacing --------------*/
max = 0;                       /*initialize max          */
for (i = 0; i < 10; i++)
    {
    if ( x[i] > max)        /*look for largest value*/
        {
        max = x[i];           /*save the new maximum  */
        isave = i;            /*and save its index    */
        }
    }

/*---another common indentation style------------*/
max = 0;                       /*initialize max          */
for (i = 0; i < 10; i++) {
    if ( x[i] > max) {      /*look for largest value*/
        max = x[i];           /*save the new maximum  */
        isave = i;            /*and save its index    */
        }
    }

/*----harder-to-read indentation and spacing---*/
max=0;
for(i=0;i<10;i++){             /*no comments either*/
if (x[i]>max)
{max=x[i];
isave=i; }
}
```

4. Avoid program "gullibility." Be sure that you do not make any unwarranted assumptions about the validity of the variables you will be working with. Don't assume that the file exists, that the value is nonzero or greater than zero, or that it is initialized. For example, the code below may not find the correct **max**

```
for (i = 0; i < 10; i++)
    {
    if ( x[i] > max)   /*look for largest value*/
        max = x[i];
    }
```

because **max** is never initialized before the search begins.

References

1. B. W. Kernighan and D.M. Ritchie, *The C Programming Language*, 2nd edition, Prentice-Hall,Englewood Cliffs, NJ, 1988.

2. A. Kelley and I. Pohl, *A Book on C,* Benjamin/Cummings, Menlo Park, NJ, 1990.

3. H. Schildt, *C Made Easy*, Osborne-McGraw-Hill, Berkeley, 1985.

4. M. Waite, S. Prata, and D. Martin, *C Primer Plus*, Howard W. Sams, Indianapolis, 1987.

5. A. Koenig, *C Traps and Pitfalls*, Addison-Wesley, Reading, MA, 1989.

THE EXAMPLE DISKETTE

If our plot complete he has managed to diskiver,
There is no retreat-- we shall certainly be hung.
The Grand Duke

The disk that accompanies this book contains an installation program that installs the program files discussed in the chapters in this book. The programs are designed for use with Borland C++ 4.0, but most can be compiled with Borland C++ version 3.1 and other standard C++ compilers such as Microsoft Visual C++. The multifile programming examples contain IDE project files used by Borland C++ 4.0 and .MAK files used for building programs with either Borland compiler.

Disk Contents

The diskette contains three installation files and a filelist.txt file containing information about the disk files. The installation program included on the diskette will install the files shown in Table 1 in subdirectories on your hard disk in a main directory called JUMPSTRT on your C: drive.

The diskette is divided into directories by chapter, and each directory contains:
- one or more example files with the **.cpp** extension,
- include files with the **.h** extension
- the Borland C++ 4.0 project files with the **.ide** extension,
- the Borland C++ make files
- the Borland C++ 4.0 desktop files with the **.dsw** extension.

Table 1. Diskette Contents by Chapter

chapter	directory	filename	purpose
3	chap3	rectangl.cpp	rectangle class

5	chap5	square.cpp	square class
6	chap6	complex0.cpp complex.cpp	two versions of complex number class
7	chap7	ios.cpp	simple **cin**, **cout** example
8	chap8	tax.cpp	income tax example
9	chap9	line.cpp	intersection of two lines
		sort.cpp	array sort program
10	chap10	fibo.cpp	Fibonacci series program
4,11,12	chap12	clstring.cpp	completed string class
13	chap13	camera.cpp betcam.cpp goodcam.cpp	camera examples showing class inheritance
		ccntrl.cpp	C-style controller function program
		cppcntrl.cpp	C++ style controller function program
14	chap14	access.cpp	demonstrates public versus private access
		auto2.cpp	autowind camera class
15	chap15	chessp.cpp pawn.cpp	chess piece class implementations
		virtual.cpp	virtual destructor example
16	chap16	concat.cpp conthis.cpp	string concatentation with and without **this** pointer
17	chap17	alliance.h busunit.h company.h conglom.h division.h	examples of business units models showing multiple inheritance
		problem1 problem2	directories of answers to exercises
18	chap18	pdemo.cpp printlib.cpp	printer classes illustrating derived classes
19	chap19	readbin.cpp writebin.cpp modify.cpp dsiplay.cpp	read, write, modify and display binary file

		box.ps	output of writeps program
		writeps.cpp	Postscript generator program
20	chap20	friend.cpp imagine.cpp	friend class and function examples
21	chap21	nearaddr.cpp	NearAddress class implementation
		static.cpp	Demonstrates using static member functions
		widget.cpp	widget class implementation
		refcount.cpp	reference counting example
22	chap22	template.cpp	template array class example
23	chap23	move1.cpp move2.cpp	demonstrates multiple base class inheritance
25	chap25	argexcpt.cpp check.cpp memexcpt.cpp nocheck.cpp	demonstrates use of exceptions
26	chap26	mkclass.cpp cmdline.cpp cppfile.cpp	complete code for **mkclass** class template generator
27	chap27	linklist.cpp	linked list example
28	chap28	stest.cpp simplex.cpp	complete simplex optimization example
29	chap29	nnetwork.cpp backprop.cpp mode.cpp nntest.cpp	neural network example
30	chap30	mset.cpp mandel.cpp	Mandelbrot fractal drawing example
	filelist.txt		complete list of files on the diskette

Making a Backup Copy

Before using the enclosed diskette, make a backup copy of the original. This backup is for personal use and will only be required in case of damage to the original. Any other use of the diskette violates copyright law.

Assuming the floppy drive you will be using is drive A:, you can make a back as follows:

1. Place the original diskette included in the book in drive A.

2. At the DOS prompt, type

```
diskcopy a: a:
```
and press Enter.

3. Wait until you are prompted to place the target diskette in drive A.

4. Remove the original diskette and replace it with you blank, backup
   ·   diskette and press Enter. The backup will continue.

5. Depending on the version of DOS, you may be prompted to re-insert the original diskette so that copying can proceed.

Installing the Diskette Files

To install the diskette files on your hard disk, you will need approximately 1 MB of free disk space. To install:

1. Place the diskette in floppy drive A and at the DOS prompt, type
   ```
   a:install
   ```
2. Follow the instructions displayed by the installation program. The default choice for the installation directory is \jumpstart and the default drive is C. At the end of the process you will be given the opportunity to review the FILELIST.TXT file for a summary of the files on the diskette.

Using the Diskette Files

In the early chapters, each **.cpp** file contains a complete example from that chapter. You can read them in to your compiler and execute them directly. In the later chapters, each example has an associated **.ide** file which contains the list of associated files which make up that solution. For these, you should select the **Project/Open** menu item and select that **.ide** file.

INDEX